WHOLE FOOD
VEGAN BAKING

WHOLE FOOD

Vegan Baking

Delicious Recipes Using Healthy, Natural Ingredients

by Annie Markowitz, PhD

ROCKRIDGE PRESS

For general information on our other products and services or to obtain technical support, please contact our Customer Care Department within the United States at (866) 744-2665, or outside the United States at (510) 253-0500.

Rockridge Press publishes its books in a variety of electronic and print formats. Some content that appears in print may not be available in electronic books, and vice versa.

Interior and Cover Designer: Heather Krakora
Art Producer: Maura Boland
Editor: Seth Schwartz
Production Manager: Riley Hoffman
Production Editor: Melissa Edeburn

Photography © 2019 Helen Dujardin. Food styling by Anna Hampton.

ISBN: Print 978-1-64611-239-5
Ebook 978-1-64611-240-1

R0

This cookbook is dedicated to my incredible parents. Without their endless, unconditional love and support, I would be nowhere near where I am today.

Contents

Introduction

Welcome to *Whole Food Vegan Baking*!

I'm Annie, and I am so glad you're here! I'm a vegan recipe blogger with a passion for all things related to food, health, and wellness.

As a teenager, and later as a college student, I struggled with my weight. I tried every diet under the sun, and nothing worked long term because I didn't enjoy eating "diet foods" and always felt restricted. Food became my enemy. I did not feel well, and I lacked energy.

I stumbled on the whole food, plant-based diet during some late-night Google searching. I began doing more and more research about the diet, browsing recipes, and I just couldn't get enough! I read stories about how eating primarily whole, plant-based foods changed people's lives by helping them lose weight, increase their energy, and reverse disease. (And the recipes looked delicious!) These benefits totally resonated with me, so I decided to give the whole food, plant-based diet a whirl. I was so excited by the fact that I could still eat brownies and lose weight! I didn't have to give up the sweets that I loved—I just had to find healthier ways to prepare them. By my third year in college, I had lost all the weight I wanted, mastered the art of vegan baking, and felt better than ever. I fell in love with food again—so much so that I went on to obtain my doctorate in nutritional sciences. My mission is to share my love for preparing delicious, nutritious vegan foods, one chocolate chip cookie at a time.

The beauty of whole foods is that they come with many powerful health benefits. Whole foods are incredibly nutritious because they are in their natural, unprocessed form, with the highest concentrations of vitamins, minerals, and antioxidants. They are also naturally high in fiber and low in sugar, and they contain gut-friendly probiotics to support digestive health. People who follow diets that are rich in whole foods have a lower risk for many diseases, including heart disease, diabetes, and cancer, and are less likely to be over- weight. Whole foods are much more filling than processed foods, thanks to their high water and fiber contents, so when you make them the center of your diet, it's much more difficult to overeat. A regular vegan diet provides many of the benefits of a whole food, plant-based diet, and it is linked with a lower risk of disease and lower rates of obesity than those associated with the standard American diet.

Now that you know all about why vegan whole foods are so good for you, you're ready to dive into this cookbook and whip up yummy and healthy vegan desserts! Baking with whole food vegan ingredients does *not* mean sacrificing taste. It simply means that you will now be able to enjoy delicious cakes, cupcakes, brownies, cookies, and more without putting anything artifi- cial into your body.

You don't have to be vegan or on the whole food, plant-based diet to enjoy the recipes in this book. These recipes are for anyone who is look- ing for amazingly flavorful yet healthy alternatives to classic sweet treats. Whether your passion is blueberry muffins, chocolate chip cookies, red velvet cupcakes, or pecan pie, this cookbook covers all your whole food vegan dessert-making needs.

WHOLE FOOD VEGAN BAKING

This cookbook features delectable baked goods that have been transformed into better-for-you versions of the classics. Each recipe uses only natural, whole food, plant-based ingredients, meaning no refined flour, no processed sugar, and no oil or butter. When you try the recipes in this cookbook, you'll be amazed at how delicious healthy baking can be. With a few easy substitutions, an oil-free vegan apple pie will have all the flavor of Grandma's original recipe, but none of the unhealthy, artery-clogging, processed ingredients. This way, you can be kind to your body while indulging in some seriously drool-worthy decadence.

Whole Food Vegan Basics

The vegan diet is made up of fruits, vegetables, nuts, seeds, and grains and excludes meat, dairy, and any other animal products. A whole food, plant-based diet is quite different. It excludes processed vegan products, from vegan sausage to vegan cheese to vegan chicken nuggets. These products are *not* whole foods and are definitely not the healthiest options. A whole food, plant-based diet is a type of vegan diet that excludes processed foods and focuses purely on natural, minimally processed foods—real foods as close as possible to their natural states.

Consuming whole foods and using whole food ingredients in cooking and baking are beneficial for many reasons. Whole foods contain tons of vitamins, minerals, antioxidants, and healthy nutrients that are stripped out of processed foods to make them more shelf stable. Whole foods are also naturally higher in fiber and lower in sugar than their processed counterparts. Fiber helps you feel full and keeps your gut happy and healthy. Increased satiety prevents overeating, so a diet rich in fiber can help you maintain a healthy weight. People who consume diets rich in whole foods tend to have less inflammation, improved heart health, and lower risks of diabetes and obesity.

Whole food vegan baking is different from conventional vegan baking in that it uses only whole food ingredients and leaves out processed and refined foods. These omissions do not have to make whole food vegan baking complicated. Just master a few simple ingredient swaps, and you'll be baking healthy, whole food treats before you know it—no additional time, work, or cleanup required.

Healthy Ingredients Matter

Common baking ingredients—all-purpose flour, butter, refined sugar, and shortening—add extra calories, fat, and sugar, which your body doesn't handle well. These ingredients can cause spikes in insulin, leaving you feeling lethargic and craving more. Luckily, there are many healthy and delicious alternatives that do not compromise flavor or texture.

In this chapter, you'll learn about the most essential whole food baking ingredient substitutions, and how to use them effectively. Plus, you'll find charts with additional ingredient substitutions on pages 92 to 93, which will come in handy when you become inspired to create your own recipes for fabulous whole food baked goods.

Whole Food Vegan Fats

Many whole food fats can be used to replace butter and oil in baked good recipes. In this book, you'll find recipes that use applesauce, pumpkin purée, nut and seed butters, and tofu as substitutes for these fats.

Applesauce is my go-to oil replacer. It works wonderfully in all baked goods—cakes, cupcakes, muffins, breads, scones, cookies, brownies, and more. Make sure you use unsweetened applesauce to avoid refined sugar. You can also make your own applesauce at home.

Pumpkin purée is another great oil replacer. It is denser than applesauce and creates a slightly heavier texture. If you aren't making your own pumpkin purée, be sure to purchase cans of 100 percent pure pumpkin purée, *not* pumpkin pie filling, which has added spices and other unnecessary ingredients. Pumpkin purée does add pumpkin flavor to baked goods, so I use it to replace the fat in pumpkin recipes only. For almost everything else, I use applesauce.

Nut and seed butters are much richer and denser than applesauce or pumpkin purée. Any type of nut butter will replace dairy butter well, but be aware that if you use peanut butter, your recipe will likely have a peanut butter flavor. Other nut and seed butters, such as almond butter and sunflower seed butter, have much subtler flavors and are not as detectable in the final product. Both store-bought and homemade nut butters work, but if you are purchasing a jar at the store, be sure that the brand you choose does not contain added sugar. I like to use nut butters to replace butter in brownies, bars, and muffins.

Tofu comes in several different textures—soft, medium firm, firm, and extra firm. The firmer the tofu, the higher the fat content. All varieties work well as butter substitutes when puréed. Soft tofu will yield the lightest and fluffiest baked goods, whereas extra firm will yield the densest. Tofu is a great ingredient to use in rich, creamy desserts, like no-bake pies, cheesecakes, and tarts.

No Oil?

Oil is extracted from plants in a process that strips out all its fiber and most of its vitamins and minerals. So although oil comes from whole foods, it is 100 percent fat—with no fiber or protein to keep you feeling full. Although olive oil and coconut oil are touted as having loads of health benefits, they are as void of nutrition as any other oil. A more nutritious way to consume healthy fats is to eat whole olives and whole coconuts. You will get all-important healthy fats, as well as receive the benefits of the rest of the whole food—fiber, protein, vitamins, and minerals.

Baking without Eggs

Baking without eggs is much easier than you might think! Eggs provide moisture, richness, structure, binding, and leavening to baked goods. There are many different whole food substitutions that can be used to replace eggs. In this book, you'll find ground flaxseed, ground chia seeds, applesauce, pumpkin purée, mashed banana, nut butters, and puréed tofu used as egg replacers.

When a traditional recipe uses eggs for binding, I turn to ground flaxseed and ground chia seeds. When you combine 1 tablespoon of either seed with 3 tablespoons of water, a gel-like consistency forms, and this mixture acts as the perfect binder in baking recipes. Ground flaxseed and ground chia seeds perform very similarly to each other in baked goods and can be used interchangeably.

Applesauce, pumpkin purée, mashed banana, and puréed soft tofu work wonderfully to replace eggs in vegan baking when the egg is there simply to provide moisture. Tofu will yield a neutral flavor, but applesauce, pumpkin purée, and mashed banana will each add a slight bit of their natural flavor to the recipe (applesauce being the subtlest). For the best results when using mashed banana, allow your bananas to turn nice and brown. If you're not ready to bake when your bananas are perfectly overripe, simply peel them and store them in a resealable bag in the freezer, then defrost as needed.

Nut butters also work well to replace the fat content of eggs. To replace 1 large egg, use any of the following ingredients/mixtures:

- 1 tablespoon ground flaxseed + 3 tablespoons water

- 1 tablespoon ground chia seeds + 3 tablespoons water

- ¼ cup puréed soft tofu

- ¼ cup unsweetened applesauce

- ¼ cup pumpkin purée

- ¼ cup mashed banana

- 3 tablespoons nut or seed butter

Baking without Milk

With various nondairy milks available in most grocery stores, it's easy to skip the dairy version in your baked goods. Any kind of nondairy milk can be used as a substitute. In this book, you'll find almond milk and coconut milk used most often.

When purchasing almond milk, check the ingredient list to make sure it's unsweetened. Either unsweetened plain or unsweetened vanilla-flavored nondairy milk will work well in the recipes in this cookbook. It doesn't matter whether you use almond milk from a shelf-stable carton or from the refrigerated section of the grocery store. Almond milk is thinner than dairy milk but thicker than water, and it has a very mild flavor that is not noticeable in baked goods.

When a recipe in this cookbook calls for coconut milk, it's referring to the coconut milk that you can purchase in a shelf-stable carton or from the refrigerated section of the grocery store. Be sure to buy unsweetened coconut milk. It is slightly thicker than almond milk and has a very subtle coconut flavor.

When you see canned light coconut milk called for in this cookbook, it's referring to cans of coconut milk that you will find in the baking section or the Asian section of your grocery store. Even the "light" version is much thicker than the type sold in a carton, and it works best in rich, creamy desserts.

Flours —

The main flours used in this book are whole wheat flour, white whole wheat flour, spelt flour, oat flour, chickpea flour, almond flour, and coconut flour. Let's take a look at these healthier-for-you flours, and what kinds of recipes they work best in.

Whole wheat flour is a hearty flour that is heavier and denser than all-purpose flour. It performs best in breads and biscuits.

White whole wheat flour and spelt flour are slightly lighter than regular whole wheat flour, and they are great for replacing all-purpose flour in most cake, cupcake, muffin, and cookie recipes. Spelt is a bit sweeter than white whole wheat and produces a spongier texture, so is best for cakes and cupcakes, although it can yield some spectacular cookies as well.

Oat flour is simply whole oats ground into a fine powder. Oat flour will make baked goods moister, fluffier, and slightly sweeter than whole wheat flour can. It's great for breads, cookies, brownies, scones, muffins, and cakes. Note that although oats are naturally gluten-free, sometimes cross-contamination can occur during production. If gluten is a concern, be sure to purchase only those brands that have the gluten-free certification on the label.

Chickpea flour, made from ground chickpeas, is another wonderful gluten-free flour. It's high in protein and quite dense, making it a powerful binder in recipes. It's great for cookies, muffins, and piecrusts.

Almond flour is made from ground blanched almonds, making it a gluten-free, higher-protein, and low-carb flour. It adds a subtle nutty, sweet flavor to baked goods. Almond flour works beautifully in muffins and scones.

Coconut flour, made from ground desiccated coconut, is another gluten-free, low-carb flour. This type of flour absorbs a lot of moisture in recipes, which can be resolved by adding extra liquid and egg replacers to prevent dryness. Coconut flour can be tricky to work with in vegan baking, so the only place you'll find it in this book is in my No-Bake Fudge Brownies (page 38).

Natural Sweeteners

Maple syrup, dates, bananas, and coconut sugar are the natural sweeteners used in this book.

Maple syrup is one of the healthiest sweeteners available. It's lower on the glycemic index than refined sugar, meaning it won't spike your blood sugar the way regular refined sugar does. It contains many essential vitamins and minerals, and it is minimally processed. It's also full of antioxidants! In baked goods, maple syrup produces a full-bodied, rich sweetness with hints of caramel and vanilla. Maple syrup is fantastic for sweetening any kind of baked goods—from breads to cookies to pies, and more! Be sure to buy pure maple syrup, not a "breakfast syrup" containing high-fructose corn syrup and all kinds of artificial ingredients.

Dates and bananas are fantastic whole food sweeteners. Dates are best used in no-bake recipes, as they act as the perfect, sticky binder. Dates mixed with nuts are the classic raw vegan piecrust—you'll find a few variations in this book! Bananas work great for adding moisture and sweetness to breads and muffins.

Coconut sugar is made from the sap of the coconut palm tree, and it makes for a delightful, minimally processed substitute for refined sugar. It can replace refined sugar in any recipe using a 1:1 ratio. Because it is less processed than white sugar, it still contains some of the vitamins, minerals, and antioxidants found in the coconut palm tree. Like maple syrup, coconut sugar is also lower on the glycemic index than refined sugar.

For those looking for a sugar-free sweetener, granulated erythritol is my favorite. It has no aftertaste or calories, and it tastes just as sweet as regular sugar. In the recipes in this book that call for coconut sugar, you swap in equal amounts of granulated erythritol.

Essential Tools

Having the right equipment can make healthy baking much more efficient and enjoyable. Here are the essential pieces of equipment used in this cookbook:

HIGH-SPEED BLENDER OR FOOD PROCESSOR. These countertop appliances are used for processing thick batters, making your own oat flour, and pulverizing raw nuts and dates.

MIXING BOWLS. You will need a few mixing bowls of various sizes to prepare dough for cookies, cakes, and more.

8-INCH SQUARE BROWNIE PAN. You will use this pan to make brownies, bars, and cakes.

9-INCH ROUND CAKE PAN. You will use this pan to make cakes and pies.

9-INCH PIE PAN. You will use this pan to make pies.

9-INCH TART PAN. You will use this pan to make pies and tarts.

7-INCH SPRINGFORM PAN. This pan has a removable bottom, which makes serving creamy pies and vegan cheesecakes much easier—and less messy.

9-BY-5-INCH LOAF PAN. You will use this pan to make quick breads and cakes.

MUFFIN TIN. You will need a standard-size 12-cup muffin tin for all the delicious muffins and cupcakes in this cookbook.

RIMMED BAKING SHEET. One or more baking sheets will help you make the cookies and scones in this cookbook.

PARCHMENT PAPER. Because there is no oil used in whole food baking, nonstick cooking spray doesn't make the cut. Parchment paper is a game-changer in oil-free baking! Every baking recipe in this cookbook requires parchment paper to prevent sticking. However, if you have nonstick bakeware, you won't need to use parchment paper.

About the Recipes

These recipes have been carefully crafted to be as healthy, easy, and delicious as possible. In each recipe, you'll find all the information you need to make it perfectly—serving size, preparation time, cook time, rest time, necessary equipment, and, of course, a no-fail, step-by-step list of detailed instructions on how to prepare the recipe.

Each recipe is labeled with its special characteristics—gluten-free, nut-free, soy-free, and no-bake—so you can be sure to choose the baked goods that are perfect for any occasion. You'll also find some great tips sprinkled throughout the cookbook, which will help you with ingredient substitutions, recipe variations, prep shortcuts, serving suggestions, storage guidelines, and more!

Now that you've learned all the basics, it's time to get over to the kitchen and get started on your whole food, plant-based baking journey! I hope you love these recipes and have a blast creating and enjoying your delicious, healthy treats. Happy baking, friends!

BREADS, BISCUITS, MUFFINS, AND SCONES

Easy Banana Bread

NUT-FREE • SOY-FREE   MAKES: 1 LOAF (10 SLICES)

PREP TIME: 10 minutes   COOK TIME: 50 minutes   COOLING TIME: 10 minutes

EQUIPMENT: 9-by-5-inch loaf pan, medium mixing bowl, large mixing bowl

When I was growing up, it was always the best day ever when my mom served me her delicious homemade banana bread for breakfast. She'd give me two little slices that I'd devour with glee before school. I'm no longer in school, but having two slices of this scrumptious, healthier banana bread for breakfast *still* makes any day the best ever!

4 overripe bananas

¼ cup unsweetened applesauce

1 teaspoon pure vanilla extract

2 cups whole wheat flour

½ cup coconut sugar

2 teaspoons baking powder

1 teaspoon ground cinnamon

½ teaspoon baking soda

¼ teaspoon salt

1. Preheat the oven to 350°F. Line a 9-by-5-inch loaf pan with parchment paper.

2. In a medium mixing bowl, mash the bananas. Add the applesauce, vanilla, and ½ cup water; mix well.

3. In a large mixing bowl, whisk together the flour, sugar, baking powder, cinnamon, baking soda, and salt.

4. Pour the wet ingredients into the dry ingredients and mix until well combined.

5. Transfer the batter to the prepared pan and bake for 40 to 50 minutes, until a toothpick inserted into the center comes out clean.

6. Remove the bread from the oven, and let it cool for 10 minutes before serving.

STORAGE: Store this bread in an airtight container or wrapped in aluminum foil in the refrigerator for up to 5 days or in the freezer for up to 3 months.

VARIATION TIP: Add 1 cup chopped nuts for some crunch and an extra nutritional boost.

Perfect Pumpkin Bread

NUT-FREE • SOY-FREE

MAKES: 1 LOAF (10 SLICES)

PREP TIME: 5 minutes

COOK TIME: 50 minutes

COOLING TIME: 10 minutes

EQUIPMENT: 9-by-5-inch loaf pan, large mixing bowl

Each year, my brothers and their families, my grandparents, and I visit my parents in beautiful Scottsdale, Arizona, to celebrate Thanksgiving. My mom always makes a few loaves of pumpkin bread for us to snack on. And because I'm her favorite daughter (aka only daughter), she always freezes an extra loaf for me to take back to Austin.

2 cups whole wheat flour

1 cup coconut sugar

2 teaspoons baking powder

½ teaspoon baking soda

1 teaspoon pumpkin pie spice

½ teaspoon salt

1 (15-ounce) can pumpkin purée

1 teaspoon pure vanilla extract

1. Preheat the oven to 350°F. Line a 9-by-5-inch loaf pan with parchment paper.

2. Combine the flour, sugar, baking powder, baking soda, pumpkin pie spice, salt, pumpkin purée, 1 cup of water, and the vanilla (in that order) in a large mixing bowl; mix well.

3. Transfer the batter to the prepared pan.

4. Bake for 40 to 50 minutes, until a toothpick inserted into the center comes out clean.

5. Remove the bread from the oven, and let it cool for 10 minutes before serving.

STORAGE: Store this bread in an airtight container or wrapped in aluminum foil in the refrigerator for up to 5 days or in the freezer for up to 3 months.

SERVING TIP: Top this loaf with Vegan Cream Cheese Frosting (page 55) for an extra delicious treat.

Gluten-Free Cinnamon-Raisin Bread

GLUTEN-FREE • NUT-FREE • SOY-FREE   MAKES: 1 LOAF (10 SLICES)

PREP TIME: 10 minutes   COOK TIME: 50 minutes   COOLING TIME: 10 minutes

EQUIPMENT: 9-by-5-inch loaf pan, medium mixing bowl, large mixing bowl

This delicious gluten-free bread tastes like an oatmeal raisin cookie. Its irresistible cinnamon flavor makes it the perfect fall treat.

1 overripe banana

1 cup unsweetened applesauce

1 teaspoon pure vanilla extract

2 cups gluten-free quick oats

1 cup coconut sugar

1 tablespoon baking powder

2 teaspoons ground cinnamon

1 cup raisins

1. Preheat the oven to 350°F. Line a 9-by-5-inch loaf pan with parchment paper.

2. In a medium mixing bowl, mash the banana. Add the applesauce, vanilla, and ½ cup water; mix well.

3. In a large mixing bowl, combine the oats, sugar, baking powder, and cinnamon and mix well.

4. Pour the wet ingredients into the dry ingredients and mix until well combined.

5. Fold in the raisins.

6. Transfer the batter to the prepared pan.

7. Bake for 40 to 50 minutes, until a toothpick inserted into the center comes out clean.

8. Remove the bread from the oven, and let it cool for 10 minutes before serving.

STORAGE: Store this bread in an airtight container or wrapped in aluminum foil in the refrigerator for up to 5 days or in the freezer for up to 3 months.

VARIATION TIP: Replace the raisins with 1 cup vegan chocolate chips to make a chocolate chip version.

10-Minute Whole Wheat Biscuits

SOY-FREE

MAKES: 5 BISCUITS

PREP TIME: 5 minutes   COOK TIME: 10 minutes   COOLING TIME: 10 minutes

EQUIPMENT: baking sheet, large mixing bowl

These tasty biscuits are so easy to make. With only one bowl and five minutes of prep time, you'll have them on the table in 20 minutes.

1 cup white whole wheat flour

1 tablespoon ground flaxseed

1½ teaspoons baking powder

¼ teaspoon garlic powder

¼ teaspoon salt

¼ cup unsweetened applesauce

¼ cup unsweetened almond milk

1. Preheat the oven to 425°F. Line a rimmed baking sheet with parchment paper.

2. In a large mixing bowl, whisk together the flour, ground flaxseed, baking powder, garlic powder, and salt.

3. Add the applesauce and almond milk and mix well.

4. Divide the dough into 5 equal pieces and form each into a square on the prepared baking sheet.

5. Bake for 8 to 10 minutes, until the edges of the biscuits are golden brown.

6. Remove the biscuits from the oven, and let them cool for 10 minutes before serving.

STORAGE: Store these biscuits in an airtight container or wrapped in aluminum foil in the refrigerator for up to 5 days or in the freezer for up to 3 months.

PREP TIP: Measure out all the dry ingredients and combine them in an airtight container ahead of time. That way, when you're in the mood for biscuits, you can just add your wet ingredients and bake.

Easy-as-Pie Apple Pie Bread

GLUTEN-FREE • NUT-FREE • SOY-FREE   MAKES: 1 LOAF (10 SLICES)

PREP TIME: 10 minutes   COOK TIME: 50 minutes   COOLING TIME: 10 minutes

EQUIPMENT: 9-by-5-inch loaf pan, large mixing bowl

This moist and delicious bread is easy to make and will fill your home with the amazing aroma of fresh-baked apple pie.

2 cups gluten-free quick oats

1 cup coconut sugar

1 tablespoon baking powder

2 teaspoons ground cinnamon

Pinch salt

1 cup unsweetened applesauce

1 teaspoon pure vanilla extract

1 large apple, such as Honeycrisp or Gala, cored and diced

1. Preheat the oven to 350°F. Line a 9-by-5-inch loaf pan with parchment paper.
2. In a large mixing bowl, whisk together the oats, sugar, baking powder, cinnamon, and salt.
3. Add the applesauce, vanilla, and ½ cup water; mix well.
4. Stir in the diced apple.
5. Transfer the batter to the prepared loaf pan.
6. Bake for 40 to 50 minutes, until a toothpick inserted into the center comes out clean.
7. Remove the bread from the oven, and let it cool for 10 minutes before serving.

STORAGE: Store this bread in an airtight container or wrapped in aluminum foil in the refrigerator for up to 5 days or in the freezer for up to 3 months.

VARIATION TIP: Replace the diced apple with 1 cup of your favorite berries to make a delicious berry version of this bread.

The Best Blueberry Muffins

GLUTEN-FREE • NUT-FREE • SOY-FREE   MAKES: 8 MUFFINS

PREP TIME: 10 minutes   COOK TIME: 20 minutes   COOLING TIME: 10 minutes

EQUIPMENT: muffin tin, blender, large mixing bowl, medium mixing bowl

These blueberry muffins are as delicious as any you can get at the grocery store—but healthier because they are made with oats.

1½ cups gluten-free quick oats

1 cup coconut sugar

1 tablespoon baking powder

Pinch salt

1 cup unsweetened applesauce

1 teaspoon pure vanilla extract

1 cup blueberries (fresh or frozen and thawed)

1. Preheat the oven to 350°F. Line 8 cups of a standard muffin tin with cupcake liners.
2. Put the quick oats in a blender and blend into a fine powder.
3. Transfer the oat flour to a large mixing bowl and add the sugar, baking powder, and salt. Whisk to combine.
4. In a medium mixing bowl, whisk together the applesauce, vanilla, and ½ cup water.
5. Pour the wet ingredients into the dry ingredients and mix well.
6. Fold in the blueberries.
7. Spoon the batter into the prepared muffin tin, filling each cupcake liner about three-quarters of the way.
8. Bake for 20 minutes or until a toothpick inserted in the center comes out clean.
9. Remove the muffins from the oven, and let them cool for 10 minutes before serving.

STORAGE: Store these muffins in an airtight container or wrapped in aluminum foil in the refrigerator for up to 5 days or in the freezer for up to 3 months.

Chickpea Flour
Chocolate Chip Muffins

GLUTEN-FREE • SOY-FREE

MAKES: 8 MUFFINS

PREP TIME: 10 minutes   COOK TIME: 25 minutes   COOLING TIME: 10 minutes

EQUIPMENT: muffin tin, blender or food processor, large mixing bowl, hand mixer

These sinfully delicious muffins are packed with fiber and protein from chickpea flour and oats to keep you feeling satisfied all morning long.

1 cup chickpea flour

½ cup gluten-free quick oats

½ cup coconut sugar

1 tablespoon ground flaxseed

1 teaspoon baking powder

1 cup unsweetened almond milk

½ cup almond butter (or other nut butter of choice)

1 teaspoon pure vanilla extract

1 cup vegan chocolate chips

1. Preheat the oven to 350°F. Line 8 cups of a standard muffin tin with cupcake liners.

2. Combine the flour, oats, sugar, ground flaxseed, and baking powder in blender or food processor; blend into a fine powder.

3. Transfer the contents of the blender or food processor to a large mixing bowl.

4. Add the almond milk, almond butter, and vanilla and use a hand mixer to mix until the batter is smooth.

5. Fold in the chocolate chips.

6. Spoon the batter into the prepared muffin tin, filling each cupcake liner about three-quarters of the way.

7. Bake for 25 minutes or until a toothpick inserted in the center comes out clean.

8. Remove the muffins from the oven, and let them cool for 10 minutes before serving.

STORAGE: Store these muffins in an airtight container or wrapped in aluminum foil in the refrigerator for up to 5 days.

Simple Banana-Nut Muffins

SOY-FREE

MAKES: 8 MUFFINS

PREP TIME: 10 minutes   COOK TIME: 18 minutes   COOLING TIME: 10 minutes

EQUIPMENT: muffin tin, small mixing bowl, medium mixing bowl, large mixing bowl

As a teenager, I used to buy banana-nut muffins from a vending machine at my high school. Here are the three things I wish I could say to my younger self: (1) These muffins are clogging your arteries. (2) You will not feel full or satisfied after eating these muffins. (3) You can easily make muffins that taste just as good but that are way better for you!

1 tablespoon ground flaxseed

3 overripe bananas

6 tablespoons pure maple syrup

¼ cup unsweetened applesauce

½ teaspoon pure vanilla extract

1 cup whole wheat flour

¼ cup quick oats

¾ teaspoon baking soda

¼ teaspoon ground cinnamon

⅛ teaspoon salt

½ cup chopped walnuts

1. Preheat the oven to 350°F. Line 8 cups of a standard muffin tin with cupcake liners.

2. In a small mixing bowl, stir the ground flaxseed into 3 tablespoons of water.

3. In a medium mixing bowl, mash the bananas. Add the maple syrup, applesauce, vanilla, and flaxseed mixture and mix well.

4. In a large mixing bowl, whisk together the flour, oats, baking soda, cinnamon, and salt.

5. Add the wet ingredients to the dry ingredients and mix well.

6. Fold in the walnuts.

7. Spoon the batter into the prepared muffin tin, filling each cupcake liner about three-quarters of the way.

(continued)

8. Bake for 16 to 18 minutes, until a toothpick inserted in the center comes out clean.

9. Remove the muffins from the oven, and let them cool for 10 minutes before serving.

STORAGE: Store these muffins in an airtight container or wrapped in aluminum foil in the refrigerator for up to 5 days or in the freezer for up to 3 months.

VARIATION TIP: This batter can also be used to make Banana-Nut Cookies. Spoon the batter into about 22 mounds on two parchment-lined rimmed baking sheets, and bake at 350°F for 15 minutes.

Double-Chocolate Muffins

SOY-FREE

MAKES: 12 MUFFINS

PREP TIME: 10 minutes   COOK TIME: 22 minutes   COOLING TIME: 30 minutes

EQUIPMENT: muffin tin, large mixing bowl

Eating chocolate for breakfast makes me feel like a rebel. These muffins are perfectly fudgy. Their brownie-like taste and texture make it hard to believe that they are actually loaded with ultra healthy ingredients.

1 cup spelt flour

1¼ cup quick oats

2 tablespoons chia seeds

½ cup cocoa powder

½ cup coconut sugar

1 teaspoon
  baking powder

½ teaspoon baking soda

Pinch salt

1 cup applesauce

1 cup almond milk

1 teaspoon vanilla extract

½ cup vegan
  chocolate chips

1. Preheat the oven to 350°F. Line 12 cups of a standard muffin tin with cupcake liners.

2. Combine flour, oats, chia seeds, cocoa powder, sugar, baking powder, baking soda, and salt in large mixing bowl and whisk.

3. Add the remaining ingredients; mix well.

4. Spoon the batter into the prepared muffin tin, filling each cupcake liner about three-quarters of the way.

5. Bake for 20 to 22 minutes, until a toothpick inserted into the center comes out clean.

6. Remove the muffins from the oven, and let them cool for at least 30 minutes before serving; they will firm up as they cool.

STORAGE: Store these muffins in an airtight container or wrapped in aluminum foil in the refrigerator for up to 5 days.

Raisin Scones

GLUTEN-FREE • SOY-FREE

MAKES: 8 SCONES

PREP TIME: 10 minutes   COOK TIME: 15 minutes   COOLING TIME: 10 minutes

EQUIPMENT: baking sheet, large mixing bowl

When I think of scones, I envision an English queen in her dining room daintily enjoying them with tea in a fine china cup. And then I look at myself "classily" burning my mouth while eating them right off the baking sheet. *That's* how good these scones are!

2 cups almond flour

2 tablespoons ground
  flaxseed

¾ teaspoon baking soda

¼ teaspoon salt

¼ cup pure maple syrup

1 teaspoon pure
  vanilla extract

½ cup raisins

1. Preheat the oven to 350°F. Line a rimmed baking sheet with parchment paper.

2. In a large mixing bowl, whisk together the flour, ground flaxseed, baking soda, and salt.

3. Add the maple syrup, vanilla, and ¼ cup water; mix well.

4. Fold in the raisins.

5. Divide the dough into 8 equal pieces and form each into a triangle on the prepared baking sheet.

6. Bake for 15 minutes or until the edges of the scones begin to brown.

7. Remove the scones from the oven, and let them cool for 10 minutes before serving.

STORAGE: Store these scones in an airtight container or wrapped in aluminum foil in the refrigerator for up to 5 days.

Blueberry Scones

GLUTEN-FREE • SOY-FREE

MAKES: 8 SCONES

PREP TIME: 10 minutes   COOK TIME: 15 minutes   COOLING TIME: 10 minutes

EQUIPMENT: baking sheet, large mixing bowl

These scones are sweet but not too sweet. They also just happen to be very easy to make—and in one bowl no less.

1 cup almond flour

1 cup gluten-free oat flour

2 tablespoons ground flaxseed

¾ teaspoon baking soda

¼ teaspoon salt

¼ cup pure maple syrup

¼ cup canned light coconut milk

1 teaspoon pure vanilla extract

½ cup blueberries (fresh or frozen and thawed)

1. Preheat the oven to 350°F. Line a rimmed baking sheet with parchment paper.

2. In a large mixing bowl, whisk together the almond flour, oat flour, ground flaxseed, baking soda, and salt.

3. Add the maple syrup, coconut milk, and vanilla; mix well.

4. Fold in the blueberries.

5. Divide the dough into 8 equal pieces and form each into a triangle on the prepared baking sheet.

6. Bake for 15 minutes or until the edges of the scones begin to brown.

7. Remove the scones from the oven, and let them cool for 10 minutes before serving.

STORAGE: Store these scones in an airtight container or wrapped in aluminum foil in the refrigerator for up to 5 days.

Chocolate Chip Scones

GLUTEN-FREE • SOY-FREE

MAKES: 8 SCONES

PREP TIME: 10 minutes   COOK TIME: 15 minutes   COOLING TIME: 10 minutes

EQUIPMENT: baking sheet, large mixing bowl

These scones are crisp on the outside and tender on the inside. They come together very easily, too. All you need is a bowl and a baking sheet.

2 cups almond flour

2 tablespoons ground flaxseed

¾ teaspoon baking soda

¼ teaspoon salt

¼ cup pure maple syrup

1 teaspoon pure vanilla extract

½ cup vegan chocolate chips

1. Preheat the oven to 350°F. Line a rimmed baking sheet with parchment paper.
2. In a large mixing bowl, whisk together the flour, ground flaxseed, baking soda, and salt.
3. Add the maple syrup, vanilla, and ¼ cup water; mix well.
4. Fold in the chocolate chips.
5. Divide the dough into 8 equal pieces and form each into a triangle on the prepared baking sheet.
6. Bake for 15 minutes or until the edges of the scones begin to brown.
7. Remove the scones from the oven, and let them cool for 10 minutes before serving.

STORAGE: Store these scones in an airtight container or wrapped in aluminum foil in the refrigerator for up to 5 days.

Pumpkin Spice Scones

GLUTEN-FREE • NUT-FREE • SOY-FREE

MAKES: 6 SCONES

PREP TIME: 10 minutes   COOK TIME: 15 minutes   COOLING TIME: 10 minutes

EQUIPMENT: baking sheet, blender or food processor

Get ready for the perfect fall breakfast treat. These scones are fluffy, moist, and absolutely delicious. Pair them with a pumpkin spice latte, and you'll be in autumn heaven all day.

2 cups gluten-free quick oats

¾ cup coconut sugar

1 tablespoon baking powder

1 teaspoon pumpkin pie spice

¼ teaspoon salt

1 (15-ounce) can pumpkin purée

1 teaspoon pure vanilla extract

1. Preheat the oven to 425°F. Line a rimmed baking sheet with parchment paper.

2. Combine all the ingredients, and ½ cup water in a blender or food processor; blend until smooth.

3. Divide the dough into 6 equal pieces and form each into a triangle on the prepared baking sheet.

4. Bake for 15 minutes or until the edges of the scones begin to brown.

5. Remove the scones from the oven, and let them cool for 10 minutes before serving.

STORAGE: Store these scones in an airtight container or wrapped in aluminum foil in the refrigerator for up to 5 days or in the freezer for up to 3 months.

VARIATION TIP: Add ½ cup vegan chocolate chips to make Chocolate Chip Pumpkin Spice Scones.

COOKIES, BROWNIES, AND BARS

The Ultimate
Chocolate Chip Cookies

GLUTEN-FREE • NUT-FREE • SOY-FREE   MAKES: 12 COOKIES

PREP TIME: 5 minutes   COOK TIME: 12 minutes   COOLING TIME: 10 minutes

EQUIPMENT: baking sheet, large mixing bowl

There's nothing like a fresh, warm chocolate chip cookie to lift your spirit. With all the flavor of a traditional chocolate chip cookie but none of the artificial or processed ingredients, this cookie is a win-win!

1 cup gluten-free oat flour

¾ cup coconut sugar

2 tablespoons ground flaxseed

1 teaspoon baking powder

¼ teaspoon salt

¼ cup unsweetened coconut milk

¼ cup unsweetened applesauce

1 teaspoon pure vanilla extract

6 tablespoons vegan chocolate chips

1. Preheat the oven to 350°F. Line a rimmed baking sheet with parchment paper.

2. In a large mixing bowl, whisk together the flour, sugar, ground flaxseed, baking powder, and salt.

3. Add the coconut milk, applesauce, and vanilla; mix well.

4. Fold in the chocolate chips.

5. Spoon the batter into 12 mounds on the prepared baking sheet.

6. Bake for 10 to 12 minutes, until the edges of the cookies begin to brown.

7. Remove the cookies from the oven, and let them cool for 10 minutes before serving.

STORAGE: Store these cookies in an airtight container or wrapped in aluminum foil in the refrigerator for up to 5 days.

VARIATION TIP: To make an oatmeal-raisin version, replace the chocolate chips with raisins and add 1 teaspoon ground cinnamon.

Oatmeal-Raisin Cookies

NUT-FREE • SOY-FREE

MAKES: 9 COOKIES

PREP TIME: 10 minutes   COOK TIME: 10 minutes   COOLING TIME: 10 minutes

EQUIPMENT: baking sheet, blender, large mixing bowl

These oatmeal-raisin cookies are soft and delicious. They're also super easy to make—just throw everything in a blender, stir in the raisins, and bake. In 10 minutes, you'll have yourself a delicious batch of healthy cookies ready to be shared.

1 cup quick oats

1 cup coconut sugar

1 cup unsweetened applesauce

½ cup white whole wheat flour

½ teaspoon baking soda

½ teaspoon ground cinnamon

½ cup raisins

1. Preheat the oven to 350°F. Line a rimmed baking sheet with parchment paper.

2. Combine the oats, sugar, applesauce, flour, baking soda, and cinnamon in a blender; blend until smooth.

3. Transfer the batter to a large mixing bowl. Fold in the raisins.

4. Spoon the batter into 9 mounds on the prepared baking sheet.

5. Bake for 10 minutes or until the edges of the cookies begin to brown.

6. Remove the cookies from the oven, and let them cool for 10 minutes before serving.

STORAGE: Store these cookies in an airtight container or wrapped in aluminum foil in the refrigerator for up to 5 days or in the freezer for up to 3 months.

VARIATION TIP: Replace the raisins with dried cranberries for a tangy twist.

Chickpea Flour
Peanut Butter Cookies

GLUTEN-FREE • SOY-FREE   MAKES: 16 COOKIES

PREP TIME: 10 minutes   REFRIGERATION TIME: 1 hour   COOK TIME: 12 minutes

COOLING TIME: 10 minutes

EQUIPMENT: large mixing bowl, small microwave-safe mixing bowl, baking sheet

As a kid, Nutter Butters were my favorite peanut butter cookie. These cookies are softer than Nutter Butters, but just as delicious. Enjoy them as is, or slather them with some peanut butter for a healthier version of those sandwich cookies from your youth.

1 cup chickpea flour

½ cup coconut sugar

1 tablespoon ground flaxseed

½ teaspoon baking soda

¼ teaspoon salt

½ cup natural peanut butter

2 tablespoons pure maple syrup

1 teaspoon pure vanilla extract

1. In a large mixing bowl, whisk together the flour, sugar, ground flaxseed, baking soda, and salt.

2. In a small microwave-safe bowl, combine the peanut butter and maple syrup. Microwave for 30 seconds to soften, then stir.

3. Add the vanilla and 2 tablespoons of water to the peanut butter mixture; whisk to combine.

4. Pour the peanut butter mixture into the bowl with the dry ingredients and mix well. Cover and refrigerate for 1 hour.

5. Preheat the oven to 350°F. Line a rimmed baking sheet with parchment paper.

6. Spoon the batter into 16 mounds on the prepared baking sheet.

7. Bake for 12 minutes or until the edges of the cookies begin to brown.

8. Remove the cookies from the oven, and let them cool for 10 minutes before serving.

STORAGE: Store these cookies in an airtight container or wrapped in aluminum foil in the refrigerator for up to 5 days.

VARIATION TIP: Add ½ cup vegan chocolate chips.

Coconut Cookies

GLUTEN-FREE • SOY-FREE   MAKES: 16 COOKIES

PREP TIME: 5 minutes   COOK TIME: 15 minutes   COOLING TIME: 15 minutes

EQUIPMENT: baking sheet, large mixing bowl

Four ingredients plus one bowl equals perfect coconut cookies—and pure happiness.

2 cups unsweetened shredded coconut

½ cup almond flour

½ cup pure maple syrup

¼ cup unsweetened applesauce

1. Preheat the oven to 350°F. Line a rimmed baking sheet with parchment paper.
2. Combine all the ingredients in a large mixing bowl; mix well.
3. Spoon the batter into 16 mounds on the prepared baking sheet.
4. Bake for about 15 minutes, until the edges of the cookies begin to brown.
5. Remove the cookies from the oven, and let them cool for 15 minutes before serving.

STORAGE: Store these cookies in an airtight container or wrapped in aluminum foil in the refrigerator for up to 5 days.

Sugar Cookies

NUT-FREE • SOY-FREE

MAKES: 18 COOKIES

PREP TIME: 5 minutes

COOK TIME: 15 minutes

COOLING TIME: 10 minutes

EQUIPMENT: baking sheet, large mixing bowl

Sometimes you need a sugar cookie—that is, a healthy sugar cookie that doesn't taste like it's healthy. Well, friends, look no further.

1¾ cups white whole wheat flour

1 cup coconut sugar

1 tablespoon ground flaxseed

1 teaspoon baking powder

½ teaspoon baking soda

¼ teaspoon salt

½ cup unsweetened applesauce

½ cup unsweetened coconut milk

1 teaspoon pure vanilla extract

1. Preheat the oven to 350°F. Line a rimmed baking sheet with parchment paper.
2. Combine all the ingredients in a large mixing bowl; mix well.
3. Spoon the batter into 18 mounds on the prepared baking sheet.
4. Bake for 10 to 15 minutes, until the edges of the cookies begin to brown.
5. Remove the cookies from the oven, and let them cool for 10 minutes before serving.

STORAGE: Store these cookies in an airtight container or wrapped in aluminum foil in the refrigerator for up to 5 days.

SUBSTITUTION TIP: You can use the same amount of oat flour in place of white whole wheat flour for a gluten-free version of this recipe.

Banana Bread Cookies

GLUTEN-FREE • NUT-FREE • SOY-FREE   MAKES: 10 COOKIES

PREP TIME: 5 minutes   COOK TIME: 15 minutes   COOLING TIME: 10 minutes

EQUIPMENT: baking sheet, large mixing bowl

This recipe requires just one bowl and 5 minutes of prep time, so you don't have to slave away in the kitchen when you feel the urge for yummy banana bread cookies. These are naturally sweetened with fruit.

2 overripe bananas

1 cup gluten-free oat flour

2 tablespoons unsweetened coconut milk

½ teaspoon ground cinnamon

½ cup raisins

1. Preheat the oven to 350°F. Line a rimmed baking sheet with parchment paper.

2. In a large mixing bowl, mash the bananas with a fork.

3. Add the flour, coconut milk, and cinnamon; mix well.

4. Fold in the raisins.

5. Spoon the batter into 10 mounds on the prepared baking sheet.

6. Bake for 15 minutes or until the edges of the cookies begin to brown.

7. Remove the cookies from the oven, and let them cool for 10 minutes before serving.

STORAGE: Store these cookies in an airtight container or wrapped in aluminum foil in the refrigerator for up to 5 days.

VARIATION TIP: You can replace the raisins with the same amount of vegan chocolate chips or chopped nuts of choice.

Pumpkin Spice Cookies

NUT-FREE • SOY-FREE

MAKES: 12 COOKIES

PREP TIME: 10 minutes   COOK TIME: 12 minutes   COOLING TIME: 10 minutes

EQUIPMENT: baking sheet, large mixing bowl

I'm a big fan of pumpkin spice *anything*. I'm also a big fan of cookies. Putting the two of them together was a no-brainer. These soft and chewy cookies will melt in your mouth.

1 cup whole wheat flour

½ cup quick oats

½ cup coconut sugar

1½ teaspoons baking powder

1 teaspoon pumpkin pie spice

¼ teaspoon salt

1 (15-ounce) can pumpkin purée

¼ cup unsweetened applesauce

½ teaspoon pure vanilla extract

1. Preheat the oven to 375°F. Line a rimmed baking sheet with parchment paper.
2. In a large mixing bowl, whisk together the flour, oats, sugar, baking powder, pumpkin pie spice, and salt.
3. Add the pumpkin purée, applesauce, vanilla, and 2 tablespoons of water; mix well.
4. Spoon the batter into 12 mounds on the prepared baking sheet.
5. Bake for 10 to 12 minutes, until the edges of the cookies begin to brown.
6. Remove the cookies from the oven, and let them cool for 10 minutes before serving.

STORAGE: Store these cookies in an airtight container or wrapped in aluminum foil in the refrigerator for up to 5 days.

VARIATION TIP: Add ½ cup unsweetened shredded coconut or chopped nuts of choice.

Cookies, Brownies, and Bars

Black Bean Brownies

GLUTEN-FREE • NUT-FREE • SOY-FREE   SERVES: 12

PREP TIME: 10 minutes   COOK TIME: 18 minutes   COOLING TIME: 15 minutes

EQUIPMENT: 8-inch square brownie pan, high-speed blender or food processor

When putting black beans in brownies and baked goods became a "thing" a few years ago, I was resistant. I was sure there was no way a brownie with *beans* in it could taste good. Well, I'm officially a believer—you cannot tell that there are beans in these fudgy brownies.

1 (15-ounce) can black beans, drained and rinsed

1 cup coconut sugar

½ cup gluten-free quick oats

¼ cup unsweetened applesauce

¼ cup unsweetened cocoa powder

2 tablespoons ground flaxseed

1½ teaspoons baking powder

1 teaspoon pure vanilla extract

½ teaspoon distilled white vinegar

1. Preheat the oven to 350°F. Line an 8-inch square brownie pan with parchment paper.
2. Combine the beans, sugar, oats, applesauce, cocoa powder, ground flaxseed, baking powder, vanilla, vinegar, and 6 tablespoons of water in a high-speed blender or food processor; blend until smooth.
3. Transfer the batter to the prepared pan.
4. Bake for 15 to 18 minutes, until a toothpick inserted into the center of the brownies comes out clean.
5. Remove the brownies from the oven, and let them cool for 15 minutes before cutting and serving.

STORAGE: Store these brownies in an airtight container or wrapped in aluminum foil in the refrigerator for up to 5 days.

SUBSTITUTION TIP: You can use chickpeas or kidney beans instead of black beans.

Scrumptious Sweet Potato Brownies

GLUTEN-FREE • NUT-FREE • SOY-FREE   SERVES: 12

PREP TIME: 10 minutes   COOK TIME: 30 minutes   COOLING TIME: 15 minutes

EQUIPMENT: 8-inch square brownie pan, high-speed blender or food processor

These brownies are delicious and nutritious. Sweet potatoes add a healthy dose of fiber, vitamins, and minerals. You'd never guess that there's a vegetable hiding in your brownies!

1 large sweet potato, cooked and mashed (about 2 cups)

½ cup gluten-free oat flour

½ cup coconut sugar

¼ cup unsweetened cocoa powder

¼ cup pure maple syrup

1 tablespoon ground flaxseed

1½ teaspoons baking powder

1. Preheat the oven to 350°F. Line an 8-inch square brownie pan with parchment paper.

2. Combine the sweet potato, flour, sugar, cocoa powder, maple syrup, ground flaxseed, baking powder, and ½ cup of water in a high-speed blender or food processor; blend until smooth.

3. Transfer the batter to the prepared pan.

4. Bake for 30 minutes or until a toothpick inserted into the center of the brownies comes out clean.

5. Remove the brownies from the oven, and let them cool for 15 minutes before cutting and serving.

STORAGE: Store these brownies in an airtight container or wrapped in aluminum foil in the refrigerator for up to 5 days.

VARIATION TIP: Add ½ cup vegan chocolate chips to make these extra chocolaty.

No-Bake Fudge Brownies

GLUTEN-FREE • SOY-FREE • NO-BAKE   SERVES: 12

PREP TIME: 10 minutes   SOAK TIME: 2 hours   REFRIGERATION TIME: 1 hour

EQUIPMENT: high-speed blender or food processor, 8-inch square brownie pan

These brownies are bursting with rich chocolate flavor. They are also very easy to make and require no baking! All you have to do is soak your dates to soften them, blend everything, transfer the batter to a brownie dish, and refrigerate for an hour.

1 cup raw walnuts

1 cup pitted dates, soaked in water for 2 hours and drained

½ cup pure maple syrup

¼ cup unsweetened cocoa powder

¼ cup unsweetened shredded coconut

3 tablespoons coconut flour

1 teaspoon pure vanilla extract

Pinch salt

1. Put the walnuts in a high-speed blender or food processor and blend until finely ground.
2. Add the dates, maple syrup, cocoa powder, shredded coconut, coconut flour, vanilla, and salt; blend until smooth.
3. Transfer the mixture to an 8-inch square brownie pan and smooth it out on top.
4. Refrigerate for at least 1 hour before cutting and serving.

STORAGE: Store these brownies in an airtight container or wrapped in aluminum foil in the refrigerator for up to 5 days or in the freezer for up to 3 months.

SUBSTITUTION TIP: You can use cashews in place of walnuts if you prefer.

Peanut Butter Swirl Brownies

GLUTEN-FREE • SOY-FREE   SERVES: 12

PREP TIME: 15 minutes   COOK TIME: 30 minutes   COOLING TIME: 15 minutes

EQUIPMENT: 8-inch square brownie pan, large mixing bowl, medium microwave-safe mixing bowl

Why choose between two of the best foods on Earth when you can have them both together? These brownies are ideal for those of us who have trouble making decisions when it comes to the important things in life, like peanut butter or chocolate.

1 cup chickpea flour

½ cup coconut sugar

¼ cup unsweetened cocoa powder

1½ teaspoons baking powder

¼ teaspoon salt

1 cup pure maple syrup, divided

½ cup unsweetened applesauce

½ cup unsweetened almond milk

1 teaspoon pure vanilla extract

¼ cup natural peanut butter

1. Preheat the oven to 350°F. Line an 8-inch square brownie pan with parchment paper.

2. In a large mixing bowl, whisk together the flour, sugar, cocoa powder, baking powder, and salt.

3. Add ¾ cup of maple syrup, the applesauce, almond milk, and vanilla; mix well. Set aside.

4. In a medium microwave-safe mixing bowl, combine the peanut butter, ¼ cup of water, and the remaining ¼ cup of maple syrup. Microwave for 30 seconds to soften, then stir.

5. Spoon half of the brownie batter into the prepared pan. Spoon half of the peanut butter mixture on top. Then, spoon the remaining brownie batter on top of the peanut butter, and finish with the remaining peanut butter mixture on top. Use a knife to make a zig-zag swirl pattern.

(continued)

6. Bake for 25 to 30 minutes, until a toothpick inserted into the center of the brownies comes out clean.

7. Remove the brownies from the oven, and let them cool for 15 minutes before cutting and serving.

STORAGE: Store these brownies in an airtight container or wrapped in aluminum foil in the refrigerator for up to 5 days.

SUBSTITUTION TIP: For a lower-fat version of this recipe, replace the peanut butter with ½ cup powdered peanut butter or peanut flour and increase the water to 6 tablespoons.

Banana-Oatmeal Breakfast Bars

GLUTEN-FREE • SOY-FREE   SERVES: 12

PREP TIME: 10 minutes   COOK TIME: 25 minutes   COOLING TIME: 15 minutes

EQUIPMENT: 8-inch square brownie pan, large mixing bowl

These oatmeal bars are basically like eating a bowl of oatmeal for breakfast, but in a much more exciting way! They taste like a treat but are packed with the goodness of oats, peanut butter, and bananas.

2 overripe bananas

1½ cups gluten-free quick oats

½ cup natural peanut butter

½ cup pure maple syrup

¼ cup unsweetened applesauce

2 tablespoons ground flaxseed

¼ teaspoon salt

1. Preheat the oven to 350°F. Line an 8-inch square brownie pan with parchment paper.

2. In a large mixing bowl, mash the bananas. Add the oats, peanut butter, maple syrup, applesauce, ground flaxseed, and salt; mix well.

3. Transfer the batter to the prepared pan.

4. Bake for 20 to 25 minutes, until a toothpick inserted into the center of the bars comes out clean.

5. Remove the pan from the oven, and let it cool for 15 minutes before cutting and serving the bars.

STORAGE: Store these bars in an airtight container or wrapped in aluminum foil in the refrigerator for up to 5 days or in the freezer for up to 3 months.

VARIATION TIP: Add ½ cup chopped peanuts or vegan chocolate chips to make these even more delicious.

Peanut Butter Cake Bars

GLUTEN-FREE • SOY-FREE

SERVES: 12

PREP TIME: 10 minutes   COOK TIME: 30 minutes   COOLING TIME: 10 minutes

EQUIPMENT: 8-inch square brownie pan, high-speed blender or food processor

Roses are red, violets are blue. I love these peanut butter cake bars, and I'm sure you will, too! With no refined sugar and plenty of wholesome oats, these cake bars are sure to become a new favorite.

1½ cups gluten-free quick oats

1 cup coconut sugar

½ cup natural peanut butter

½ cup unsweetened applesauce

1 tablespoon ground flaxseed

2 teaspoons pure vanilla extract

1½ teaspoons baking powder

¼ teaspoon salt

1. Preheat the oven to 350°F. Line an 8-inch square brownie pan with parchment paper.

2. Combine the oats, sugar, peanut butter, applesauce, ground flaxseed, vanilla, baking powder, salt, and ¾ cup of water in a high-speed blender or food processor; blend until smooth.

3. Transfer the batter to the prepared pan.

4. Bake for 30 minutes or until a toothpick inserted into the center of the bars comes out clean.

5. Remove the cake from the oven, and let it cool for 10 minutes before cutting and serving.

STORAGE: Store these bars in an airtight container or wrapped in aluminum foil in the refrigerator for up to 5 days or in the freezer for up to 3 months.

Oatmeal–Chocolate Chip Cookie Bars

GLUTEN-FREE • NUT-FREE • SOY-FREE   SERVES: 12

PREP TIME: 10 minutes   COOK TIME: 25 minutes   COOLING TIME: 10 minutes

EQUIPMENT: 8-inch square brownie pan, large mixing bowl

I've always loved sweets for breakfast. I would take a pastry over a (vegan) omelet and tofu bacon any day! Even though these bars look and taste like dessert, they are nutritious enough to make for a healthy start to your day. I like to make a big batch on Sunday so that I can enjoy them all week long.

1½ cups gluten-free quick oats

1 cup coconut sugar

½ cup unsweetened applesauce

½ cup water or unsweetened coconut milk

2 tablespoons ground flaxseed

1 teaspoon pure vanilla extract

¼ teaspoon salt

½ cup vegan chocolate chips

1. Preheat the oven to 350°F. Line an 8-inch square brownie pan with parchment paper.

2. In a large mixing bowl, combine the oats, sugar, applesauce, water or unsweetened coconut milk, ground flaxseed, vanilla, and salt; mix well.

3. Fold in the chocolate chips.

4. Transfer the batter to the prepared pan.

5. Bake for 20 to 25 minutes, until a toothpick inserted into the center of the bars comes out clean.

6. Remove the cookie from the oven, and let it cool for 10 minutes before cutting and serving.

STORAGE: Store these bars in an airtight container or wrapped in aluminum foil in the refrigerator for up to 5 days or in the freezer for up to 3 months.

VARIATION TIP: Add an additional ½ cup vegan chocolate chips or ½ cup chopped nuts of choice to make these even more decadent.

Chocolate Chip Cookie Dough Bars

GLUTEN-FREE • SOY-FREE   SERVES: 12

PREP TIME: 10 minutes   COOK TIME: 30 minutes   COOLING TIME: 10 minutes

EQUIPMENT: 8-inch square brownie pan, high-speed blender or food processor, large mixing bowl

Though baked, these bars come out of the oven soft and gooey like cookie dough.

1 (15-ounce) can chickpeas, drained and rinsed

½ cup coconut sugar

½ cup gluten-free quick oats

½ cup pure maple syrup

½ cup unsweetened coconut milk

¼ cup natural peanut butter

¼ cup unsweetened applesauce

1 teaspoon pure vanilla extract

¾ teaspoon baking powder

⅛ teaspoon baking soda

½ cup vegan chocolate chips

1. Preheat the oven to 350°F. Line an 8-inch square brownie pan with parchment paper.

2. Combine the chickpeas, sugar, oats, maple syrup, coconut milk, peanut butter, apple-sauce, vanilla, baking powder, and baking soda in a high-speed blender or food processor; blend until smooth.

3. Transfer the batter to a large mixing bowl.

4. Fold in the chocolate chips.

5. Transfer the batter to the prepared pan.

6. Bake for 30 minutes or until a toothpick inserted into the center of the bars comes out mostly clean (a little residue is fine).

7. Remove the bars from the oven, and let them cool for 10 minutes before cutting and serving.

STORAGE: Store these bars in an airtight container or wrapped in aluminum foil in the refrigerator for up to 5 days.

Strawberry Oatmeal Bars

GLUTEN-FREE • NUT-FREE • SOY-FREE   SERVES: 12

PREP TIME: 10 minutes   COOK TIME: 40 minutes   COOLING TIME: 15 minutes

EQUIPMENT: 8-inch square brownie pan, large mixing bowl

These bars are a perfect summer dessert—but so healthy that they can be eaten for breakfast. They feature two superstar ingredients: The first is oats, which are high in fiber to keep you feeling satiated for hours, and the second is strawberries, which are loaded with vitamins and antioxidants.

1½ cups gluten-free quick oats

1 cup coconut sugar

½ cup pure maple syrup

½ cup unsweetened applesauce

1½ teaspoons baking powder

1 teaspoon pure vanilla extract

¼ teaspoon salt

1 cup sliced strawberries

1. Preheat the oven to 350°F. Line an 8-inch square brownie pan with parchment paper.

2. In a large mixing bowl, combine the oats, sugar, maple syrup, applesauce, baking powder, vanilla, salt, and 6 tablespoons of water; mix well.

3. Fold in the sliced strawberries.

4. Transfer the batter to the prepared pan.

5. Bake for 30 to 40 minutes, until a toothpick inserted into the center of the bars comes out clean.

6. Remove the pan from the oven, and let it cool for 15 minutes before cutting and serving the bars.

STORAGE: Store these bars in an airtight container or wrapped in aluminum foil in the refrigerator for up to 5 days.

VARIATION TIP: Use any kind of fruit in place of the strawberries to turn these into the fruit bar of your choice. I've tried this recipe with peaches and blueberries, and both variations were delicious.

Cookies, Brownies, and Bars

Peanut Butter Granola Bars with Chocolate Drizzle

GLUTEN-FREE • SOY-FREE   SERVES: 8

PREP TIME: 10 minutes   COOK TIME: 20 minutes   COOLING TIME: 10 minutes

EQUIPMENT: 9-by-5-inch loaf pan, large mixing bowl, small mixing bowl

Made with whole food ingredients and without processed sugar, butter, or oil, these bars are a deliciously satisfying grab-and-go snack.

FOR THE GRANOLA BARS

1¼ cups gluten-free quick oats

¼ cup pure maple syrup

2 tablespoons unsweetened applesauce

2 tablespoons natural peanut butter

2 tablespoons coconut sugar

2 tablespoons chopped peanuts

½ teaspoon pure vanilla extract

Pinch salt

1. Preheat the oven to 325°F. Line a 9-by-5-inch loaf pan with parchment paper.

2. To make the granola bars: In a large mixing bowl, combine all the granola bar ingredients and mix well.

3. Spoon the mixture into the prepared loaf pan and press down to smooth the top.

4. To make the chocolate drizzle: In a small mixing bowl, whisk together the cocoa powder, maple syrup, salt, and 1 tablespoon of water.

2 tablespoons
   unsweetened
   .cocoa powder

2 tablespoons pure
   maple syrup

Pinch salt

5. Drizzle the mixture on top of the granola batter.

6. Bake for 15 to 20 minutes, until a toothpick inserted into the center comes out clean.

7. Remove the pan from the oven, and let it cool for 10 minutes before cutting and serving the bars.

STORAGE: Store these bars in an airtight container or wrapped in aluminum foil in the refrigerator for up to 5 days or in the freezer for up to 3 months.

Cookies, Brownies, and Bars

CAKES AND CUPCAKES

Classic Vanilla Cake with Low-Fat Vanilla Frosting

NUT-FREE • SOY-FREE   SERVES: 8

PREP TIME: 10 minutes   COOK TIME: 25 minutes   COOLING TIME: 30 minutes

EQUIPMENT: 9-inch round cake pan, blender, large mixing bowl

Everyone needs a go-to, no-fail cake recipe, and this is mine. It's what I make for birthdays, and it's always a hit.

FOR THE CAKE

1 cup white whole wheat flour

1 cup gluten-free quick oats

¾ cup coconut sugar

1½ tablespoons baking powder

¼ teaspoon salt

½ cup pure maple syrup

½ cup unsweetened applesauce

2 teaspoons pure vanilla extract

1. Preheat the oven to 350°F. Line a 9-inch round cake pan with parchment paper.

2. To make the cake: Combine the flour, oats, sugar, baking powder, and salt in a blender; blend into a fine powder.

3. Transfer the contents of the blender to a large mixing bowl.

4. Add the maple syrup, applesauce, vanilla, and ½ cup of water; mix well.

5. Transfer the batter to the prepared pan and bake for 20 to 25 minutes, until a toothpick inserted into the center of the cake comes out clean. Set aside until completely cooled, about 30 minutes.

FOR THE FROSTING

1 cup mashed cooked
   white sweet potato
   (about ½ large
   sweet potato)

½ cup pure maple syrup

2 tablespoons
   coconut sugar

1 teaspoon freshly
   squeezed lemon juice

1 teaspoon pure
   vanilla extract

Pinch salt

6. While the cake is baking, combine all the frosting ingredients in the blender and blend until smooth. Cover and refrigerate for 30 minutes to thicken.

7. Once the cake has cooled, frost and enjoy.

STORAGE: Store this cake in an airtight container in the refrigerator for up to 5 days.

SUBSTITUTION TIP: A regular white potato can also be used for the frosting, but you will need to add additional sweetener to taste. You can also use a regular orange sweet potato, but the frosting will be orange!

Dad's Decadent Chocolate Cake with Low-Fat Chocolate Frosting

GLUTEN-FREE • NUT-FREE • SOY-FREE   SERVES: 8

PREP TIME: 10 minutes   COOK TIME: 25 minutes   COOLING TIME: 30 minutes

EQUIPMENT: 9-inch round cake pan, blender

My dad is *not* a sweets guy. The only dessert I've ever seen him eat is this chocolate cake. When the guy who doesn't like sweets likes a cake, you know it's good.

FOR THE CAKE

2 cups gluten-free quick oats

¾ cup coconut sugar

½ cup unsweetened cocoa powder

½ cup pure maple syrup

½ cup unsweetened applesauce

½ cup canned light coconut milk

1 tablespoon apple cider vinegar

2 teaspoons pure vanilla extract

1 teaspoon instant coffee powder (optional)

1 teaspoon baking powder

½ teaspoon baking soda

¼ teaspoon salt

1. Preheat the oven to 350°F. Line a 9-inch round cake pan with parchment paper.

2. To make the cake: Combine all the cake ingredients in a blender and blend until smooth.

3. Transfer the batter to the prepared cake pan.

4. Bake for 20 to 25 minutes, until a toothpick inserted into the center of the cake comes out clean. Set aside until completely cooled, about 30 minutes.

1 cup mashed cooked white sweet potato (about ½ large sweet potato)

½ cup pure maple syrup

2 tablespoons coconut sugar

2 teaspoons unsweetened cocoa powder

1 teaspoon freshly squeezed lemon juice

1 teaspoon pure vanilla extract

¼ teaspoon instant coffee powder

Pinch salt

5. While the cake is baking, combine all the frosting ingredients in the blender and blend until smooth. Cover and refrigerate for 30 minutes to thicken.

6. Once the cake has cooled, frost and enjoy.

STORAGE: Store this cake in an airtight container in the refrigerator for up to 5 days.

Healthy Carrot Cake with Vegan Cream Cheese Frosting

NUT-FREE SERVES: 12

PREP TIME: 15 minutes   COOK TIME: 45 minutes   COOLING TIME: 30 minutes

EQUIPMENT: 9-by-5-inch loaf pan, large mixing bowl, blender

When I think of carrots, I think of bunnies and of watching Bugs Bunny cartoons as a child. The only thing that would have made my eight-year-old self any happier is a big slice of this carrot cake!

FOR THE CAKE

2 cups spelt flour

⅓ cup coconut sugar

2 tablespoons ground flaxseed

2 teaspoons ground cinnamon

1½ teaspoons baking powder

½ teaspoon baking soda

½ teaspoon ground ginger

¼ teaspoon ground nutmeg

¼ teaspoon salt

½ cup pure maple syrup

½ cup unsweetened applesauce

1 tablespoon apple cider vinegar

2 teaspoons pure vanilla extract

1 tablespoon freshly squeezed lemon juice

1½ cups shredded carrots

1. Preheat the oven to 350°F. Line a 9-by-5-inch loaf pan with parchment paper.
2. To make the cake: In a large mixing bowl, whisk together the flour, sugar, ground flaxseed, cinnamon, baking powder, baking soda, ginger, nutmeg, and salt.
3. Add the maple syrup, applesauce, apple cider vinegar, vanilla, and lemon juice; mix well.
4. Fold in the shredded carrots.
5. Transfer the batter to the prepared pan.

1 (14-ounce) block firm
   tofu, drained

6 tablespoons
   coconut sugar

¼ cup pure maple syrup

2 tablespoons plus
   1 teaspoon freshly
   squeezed lemon juice

1 tablespoon pure
   vanilla extract

1 tablespoon apple
   cider vinegar

⅛ teaspoon salt

6. Bake for 40 to 45 minutes, until a toothpick inserted into the center of the cake comes out clean. Set aside until completely cooled, about 30 minutes.

7. While the cake is baking, combine all the frosting ingredients in a blender and blend until smooth.

8. Once the cake has cooled, frost and enjoy.

STORAGE: Store this cake in an airtight container in the refrigerator for up to 5 days.

VARIATION TIP: Add ½ cup chopped walnuts, chopped pecans, or slivered almonds to the batter.

Simple Banana Cake

NUT-FREE • SOY-FREE   SERVES: 12

PREP TIME: 10 minutes   COOK TIME: 30 minutes   COOLING TIME: 15 minutes

EQUIPMENT: 8-inch square brownie pan, blender

This cake is perfectly fluffy and moist. Made with whole grains and oats, it's also super healthy.

3 overripe bananas

1 cup spelt flour

1 cup quick oats

½ cup coconut sugar

½ cup unsweetened applesauce

¼ cup pure maple syrup

1½ teaspoons baking powder

1 teaspoon ground cinnamon

1 teaspoon pure vanilla extract

¼ teaspoon salt

1. Preheat the oven to 350°F. Line an 8-inch square brownie pan with parchment paper.

2. Combine the bananas, flour, oats, sugar, applesauce, maple syrup, baking powder, cinnamon, vanilla, salt, and ¾ cup of water in a blender; blend until smooth.

3. Transfer the batter to the prepared pan.

4. Bake for 25 to 30 minutes, until a toothpick inserted into the center of the cake comes out clean.

5. Remove the cake from the oven, and let it cool for 15 minutes before slicing and serving.

STORAGE: Store this cake in an airtight container or wrapped in aluminum foil in the refrigerator for up to 5 days.

VARIATION TIP: Add 1 cup chopped walnuts to the batter for a delicious banana nut cake!

Chocolate Chip Cookie Cake

NUT-FREE • SOY-FREE

SERVES: 8

PREP TIME: 10 minutes

COOK TIME: 25 minutes

COOLING TIME: 15 minutes

EQUIPMENT: 9-inch round cake pan, large mixing bowl

Which is better: cake or cookie cake? If you ask me, it's cookie cake. This cookie cake is not just delicious and healthy. It's also easy to make.

2 cups white whole wheat flour

¾ cup coconut sugar

½ cup pure maple syrup

½ cup unsweetened applesauce

½ cup unsweetened coconut milk

1½ tablespoons baking powder

2 teaspoons pure vanilla extract

¼ teaspoon salt

¾ cup vegan chocolate chips

1. Preheat the oven to 350°F. Line a 9-inch round cake pan with parchment paper.

2. In a large mixing bowl, combine the flour, sugar, maple syrup, applesauce, coconut milk, baking powder, vanilla, and salt; mix well.

3. Fold in the chocolate chips.

4. Transfer the batter to the prepared pan.

5. Bake for 20 to 25 minutes, until a toothpick inserted into the center of the cake comes out clean.

6. Remove the cake from the oven, and let it cool for 15 minutes before slicing and serving.

STORAGE: Store this cake in an airtight container or wrapped in aluminum foil in the refrigerator for up to 5 days.

Lemon–Poppy Seed Cake

NUT-FREE • SOY-FREE   SERVES: 12

PREP TIME: 10 minutes   COOK TIME: 30 minutes   COOLING TIME: 30 minutes

EQUIPMENT: 8-inch square brownie pan, blender, large mixing bowl

This cake is moist, sweet, lemon perfection.

1 cup quick oats

¾ cup coconut sugar

½ cup white whole
   wheat flour

2 teaspoons ground
   cinnamon

1 teaspoon
   baking powder

½ teaspoon baking soda

¼ teaspoon salt

Grated zest of 1 lemon

½ cup freshly squeezed
   lemon juice

½ cup unsweetened
   coconut milk

¼ cup pure maple syrup

¼ cup unsweetened
   applesauce

1 teaspoon pure
   vanilla extract

2 tablespoons
   poppy seeds

1. Preheat the oven to 350°F. Line an 8-inch square brownie pan with parchment paper.

2. Combine the oats, sugar, flour, cinnamon, baking powder, baking soda, and salt in a blender; blend into a fine powder.

3. Transfer the contents of the blender to a large mixing bowl.

4. Add the lemon zest and juice, coconut milk, maple syrup, applesauce, and vanilla; mix well.

5. Stir in the poppy seeds.

6. Transfer the batter to the prepared pan.

7. Bake for 25 to 30 minutes, until a toothpick inserted into the center of the cake comes out clean.

8. Remove the cake from the oven, and let it cool for 30 minutes before slicing and serving.

STORAGE: Store this cake in an airtight container or wrapped in aluminum foil in the refrigerator for up to 5 days.

SERVING TIP: Top this cake with Low-Fat Vanilla Frosting (page 51), Creamy Vanilla Frosting (page 62), or Vegan Cream Cheese Frosting (page 55).

The Best Coffee Cake

NUT-FREE • SOY-FREE   SERVES: 12

PREP TIME: 10 minutes   COOK TIME: 30 minutes   COOLING TIME: 15 minutes

EQUIPMENT: 8-inch square brownie pan, large mixing bowl, small mixing bowl

This cake is flavored with spices reminiscent of pumpkin pie. Enjoy with (or without) your favorite hot beverage.

FOR THE CAKE

1 cup quick oats

¾ cup coconut sugar

½ cup white whole wheat flour

2 teaspoons ground cinnamon

2 teaspoons ground ginger

1 teaspoon ground nutmeg

1 teaspoon baking powder

½ teaspoon baking soda

¼ teaspoon salt

½ cup pure maple syrup

½ cup unsweetened applesauce

¼ cup canned light coconut milk

2 teaspoons pure vanilla extract

1. Preheat the oven to 350°F. Line an 8-inch square brownie pan with parchment paper.

2. Combine the oats, sugar, flour, cinnamon, ginger, nutmeg, baking powder, baking soda, and salt in a blender; blend into a fine powder.

3. Transfer the contents of the blender to a large mixing bowl.

4. Add the maple syrup, applesauce, coconut milk, vanilla, and ¼ cup of water; mix well.

5. Transfer the batter to the prepared pan.

(continued)

Cakes and Cupcakes

FOR THE TOPPING

½ cup coconut sugar

6 tablespoons oat flour

2 tablespoons unsweetened applesauce

½ teaspoon ground cinnamon

6. In a small mixing bowl, combine all the topping ingredients and mix well.

7. Spoon the topping mixture on top of the batter.

8. Bake for 25 to 30 minutes, until a toothpick inserted into the center of the cake comes out clean.

9. Remove the cake from the oven, and let it cool for 15 minutes before slicing and serving.

STORAGE: Store this cake in an airtight container or wrapped in aluminum foil in the refrigerator for up to 5 days.

Jasmine's Vanilla Cupcakes with Creamy Vanilla Frosting

NUT-FREE   SERVES: 8

PREP TIME: 10 minutes   COOK TIME: 13 minutes   COOLING TIME: 30 minutes

EQUIPMENT: muffin tin, large mixing bowl, blender

I'm always eager to show my friends and family how delicious my healthy versions of baked goods can be. When I learned that vanilla cupcakes are the favorite dessert of my dear friend Jasmine, it became my mission to create the perfect cupcake for her. Well, friends, it worked—she loves these vanilla cupcakes, and so will you!

FOR THE CUPCAKES

1 cup white whole wheat flour

½ cup coconut sugar

½ cup unsweetened applesauce

5 tablespoons pure maple syrup

1 teaspoon apple cider vinegar

1 teaspoon pure vanilla extract

1 teaspoon baking powder

⅛ teaspoon salt

1. Preheat the oven to 350°F. Line 8 cups of a standard muffin tin with cupcake liners.

2. To make the cupcakes: In a large mixing bowl, combine the flour, sugar, applesauce, maple syrup, vinegar, vanilla, baking powder, salt, and ½ cup of water; mix well.

3. Spoon the batter into the prepared muffin tin, filling each cupcake liner about three-quarters of the way.

4. Bake for 11 to 13 minutes, until a toothpick inserted into the center of a cupcake comes out clean. Set aside until completely cooled, about 30 minutes.

(continued)

FOR THE FROSTING

1 (14-ounce) block firm
  tofu, drained

6 tablespoons
  coconut sugar

¼ cup pure maple syrup

2 tablespoons plus
  1 teaspoon freshly
  squeezed lemon juice

1 tablespoon pure
  vanilla extract

⅛ teaspoon salt

5. While the cupcakes are baking, combine all the frosting ingredients in a blender and blend until smooth. Cover and refrigerate for 30 minutes to thicken.

6. Once the cupcakes have cooled, frost and enjoy.

STORAGE: Store these cupcakes in an airtight container in the refrigerator for up to 5 days.

SUBSTITUTION TIP: Use Chocolate–Peanut Butter Frosting (page 64) instead of vanilla for a delicious twist.

Chocolate Cupcakes with Chocolate–Peanut Butter Frosting

SOY-FREE   SERVES: 12

PREP TIME: 10 minutes   COOK TIME: 18 minutes   COOLING TIME: 30 minutes

EQUIPMENT: muffin tin, large mixing bowl, small mixing bowl, medium microwave-safe mixing bowl

Did I want chocolate or vanilla cupcakes for my birthday? As a child, this decision was a *very* big one. Chocolate almost always won. These chocolate cupcakes are just as delicious as the ones of my youth, but without all the fat, calories, and refined sugar.

FOR THE CUPCAKES

1 cup white whole wheat flour

1 cup coconut sugar

¼ cup unsweetened cocoa powder

½ teaspoon baking powder

Pinch salt

¼ cup pure maple syrup

1 teaspoon apple cider vinegar

1 teaspoon pure vanilla extract

1. Preheat the oven to 350°F. Line a standard muffin tin with cupcake liners.

2. To make the cupcakes: In a large mixing bowl, whisk together the flour, sugar, cocoa powder, baking powder, and salt.

3. In a small mixing bowl, whisk together the maple syrup, vinegar, and vanilla.

4. Pour the wet ingredients into the bowl with the dry ingredients and mix well.

5. Spoon the mixture into the prepared muffin tin, filling each cupcake liner about three-quarters of the way.

6. Bake for 15 to 18 minutes, until a toothpick inserted into the center of a cupcake comes out clean. Set aside until completely cooled, about 30 minutes.

(continued)

FOR THE FROSTING

¾ cup pure maple syrup

½ cup natural
  peanut butter

6 tablespoons
  unsweetened
  almond milk

½ cup unsweetened
  cocoa powder

7. While the cupcakes are baking, make the frosting: In a medium microwave-safe mixing bowl, combine the maple syrup, peanut butter, and almond milk. Microwave for 30 seconds to soften, then stir.

8. Add the cocoa powder and mix well. Cover and refrigerate for 30 minutes to thicken.

9. Once the cupcakes have cooled, frost and enjoy.

STORAGE: Store these cupcakes in an airtight container in the refrigerator for up to 5 days.

VARIATION TIP: Use almond butter or cashew butter in place of the peanut butter to switch up the flavor of the frosting.

Red Velvet Cupcakes with Vegan Cream Cheese Frosting

NUT-FREE

PREP TIME: 15 minutes   COOK TIME: 25 minutes

SERVES: 8

COOLING TIME: 30 minutes

EQUIPMENT: muffin tin, high-speed blender or food processor, large mixing bowl, small mixing bowl

Having trouble deciding between chocolate and vanilla cupcakes? Try these red velvet ones instead.

FOR THE CUPCAKES

1 cup white whole wheat flour

½ cup coconut sugar

¼ cup unsweetened cocoa powder

1 teaspoon baking powder

½ teaspoon baking soda

⅛ teaspoon salt

1 small beet, cubed

½ cup unsweetened applesauce

5 tablespoons pure maple syrup

1 teaspoon pure vanilla extract

1 teaspoon apple cider vinegar

1. Preheat the oven to 350°F. Line 8 cups of a standard muffin tin with cupcake liners.

2. In a large mixing bowl, whisk together the flour, sugar, cocoa powder, baking powder, baking soda, and salt.

3. Combine the beet, applesauce, maple syrup, vanilla, vinegar, and ½ cup of water in a high-speed blender or food processor; blend until smooth.

4. Pour the contents of the blender into the dry ingredients and mix well.

5. Spoon the batter into the prepared muffin tin, filling each cupcake liner about three-quarters of the way.

6. Bake for 20 to 25 minutes, until a toothpick inserted into the center of a cupcake comes out clean. Set aside until completely cooled, about 30 minutes.

(continued)

FOR THE FROSTING

1 (14-ounce) block firm
   tofu, drained

6 tablespoons
   coconut sugar

¼ cup pure maple syrup

2 tablespoons plus
   1 teaspoon freshly
   squeezed lemon juice

1 tablespoon pure
   vanilla extract

1 tablespoon apple
   cider vinegar

⅛ teaspoon salt

7. While the cupcakes are baking, combine all the frosting ingredients in the blender and blend until smooth. Cover and refrigerate for at least 30 minutes to thicken.

8. Once the cupcakes have cooled, frost and enjoy.

STORAGE: Store these cupcakes in an airtight container in the refrigerator for up to 5 days.

VARIATION TIP: Add ½ cup vegan chocolate chips to the batter to make these cupcakes even more decadent.

Mixed Berry Cake

SOY-FREE   SERVES: 8

PREP TIME: 10 minutes   COOK TIME: 25 minutes   COOLING TIME: 30 minutes

EQUIPMENT: 9-inch round cake pan, blender, large mixing bowl

This is the perfect cake for summer, when fresh berries are plentiful. It's so pretty and colorful, it's guaranteed to bring a smile to your face.

1 cup white whole wheat flour

1 cup quick oats

¾ cup coconut sugar

1½ tablespoons baking powder

¼ teaspoon salt

½ cup pure maple syrup

½ cup unsweetened applesauce

2 teaspoons pure vanilla extract

1 cup mixed berries

1. Preheat the oven to 350°F. Line a 9-inch round cake pan with parchment paper.

2. Combine the flour, oats, sugar, baking powder, and salt in a blender; blend into a fine powder.

3. Transfer the contents of the blender to a large mixing bowl.

4. Add the maple syrup, applesauce, vanilla, and ½ cup of water; mix well.

5. Fold in the berries.

6. Transfer the batter to the prepared cake pan.

7. Bake for 20 to 25 minutes, until a toothpick inserted into the center of the cake comes out clean.

8. Remove the cake from the oven, and let it cool for 30 minutes before slicing and serving.

STORAGE: Store this cake in an airtight container or wrapped in aluminum foil in the refrigerator for up to 5 days.

VARIATION TIP: You can make this recipe using peaches or apples instead of berries—or try pineapple for a tropical twist.

No-Bake Vegan Cheesecake

GLUTEN-FREE • SOY-FREE • NO-BAKE   SERVES: 8

PREP TIME: 10 minutes   FREEZE TIME: 6 hours   DEFROST TIME: 20 minutes

EQUIPMENT: 7-inch springform pan, high-speed blender or food processor

This raw vegan cheesecake doesn't require baking. Just blend every-thing, transfer the batter to a springform pan, and pop it in the freezer. The result is rich and decadent.

FOR THE CRUST

1 cup raw cashews

½ cup raw walnuts

¼ cup pure maple syrup

Pinch salt

FOR THE FILLING

2 cups raw cashews, soaked in water for 2 hours, then drained

½ cup unsweetened applesauce

½ cup pure maple syrup

4 pitted dates

3 tablespoons freshly squeezed lemon juice

½ teaspoon pure vanilla extract

¼ teaspoon salt

1. Line a 7-inch springform pan with parchment paper.

2. To make the crust: Combine the cashews, walnuts, maple syrup, and salt in a high-speed blender or food processor; blend until everything is well combined.

3. Transfer the crust mixture to the prepared pan, and use a spatula to press it down evenly into the bottom of the pan.

4. To make the filling: Combine the cashews, applesauce, maple syrup, dates, lemon juice, vanilla, and salt in the blender or food processor; blend until smooth.

5. Spoon the filling mixture onto the crust and smooth the top.

6. Cover and freeze for at least 6 hours.

7. Transfer the cheesecake to the refrigerator 20 minutes before you'd like to serve it. If you like it even softer, continue to let defrost until the desired consistency is achieved.

STORAGE: Store this cake in an airtight container or wrapped in aluminum foil in the freezer for up to 3 months.

SERVING TIP: Serve with fresh berries and vegan whipped cream.

PIES AND TARTS

Dreamy Chocolate Silk Pie

GLUTEN-FREE • NO-BAKE   SERVES: 8

PREP TIME: 15 minutes   FREEZE TIME: 6 hours   DEFROST TIME: 1 hour

EQUIPMENT: 7-inch springform pan, high-speed blender or food processor

This decadent pie boasts a creamy chocolate filling and a chocolate-nut crust. It's super easy to make and requires no baking.

FOR THE CRUST

1 cup raw cashews

½ cup raw walnuts

¼ cup pure maple syrup

2 tablespoons unsweetened cocoa powder

FOR THE FILLING

½ (14-ounce) block medium firm tofu, drained

1 cup raw cashews

¾ cup coconut sugar

¼ cup pure maple syrup

¼ cup canned light coconut milk

¼ cup unsweetened cocoa powder

1 teaspoon pure vanilla extract

1. Line a 7-inch springform pan with parchment paper.

2. To make the crust: Combine the cashews, walnuts, maple syrup, and cocoa powder in a high-speed blender or food processor; blend until everything is well combined.

3. Transfer the crust mixture to the prepared pan, and use a spatula to press it down evenly into the bottom of the pan.

4. To make the filling: Combine the tofu, cashews, sugar, maple syrup, coconut milk, cocoa powder, vanilla, and ¼ cup of water in the blender or food processor; blend until smooth.

5. Spoon the filling mixture onto the crust.

6. Cover and freeze for at least 6 hours.

7. Take the cheesecake out of the freezer 1 hour before you'd like to serve it. If you like it even softer, continue to let defrost until the desired consistency is achieved.

STORAGE: Store this pie in an airtight container or wrapped in aluminum foil in the freezer for up to 3 months.

VARIATION TIP: Add ½ cup vegan chocolate chips to the pie filling for even more chocolaty goodness.

No-Bake Creamy Peanut Butter Mousse Pie

GLUTEN-FREE • NO-BAKE   SERVES: 8

PREP TIME: 15 minutes   FREEZE TIME: 6 hours   DEFROST TIME: 1 hour

EQUIPMENT: 7-inch springform pan, high-speed blender or food processor

If I were stranded on a desert island and allowed to have only one food, it would definitely be peanut butter. I would be lying if I told you that I've never eaten this pie for breakfast.

FOR THE CRUST

1 cup raw cashews

½ cup raw walnuts

¼ cup pure maple syrup

Pinch salt

FOR THE FILLING

½ (14-ounce) block medium firm tofu, drained

¾ cup coconut sugar

½ cup canned chickpeas

½ cup raw cashews

6 tablespoons natural peanut butter

¼ cup pure maple syrup

¼ cup canned light coconut milk

1 teaspoon pure vanilla extract

Pinch salt

1. Line a 7-inch springform pan with parchment paper.

2. To make the crust: Combine the cashews, walnuts, maple syrup, and salt in a high-speed blender or food processor; blend until the ingredients are well combined.

3. Transfer the crust mixture to the prepared pan, and use a spatula to press it down evenly into the bottom of the pan.

4. To make the filling: Combine the tofu, sugar, chickpeas, cashews, peanut butter, maple syrup, coconut milk, vanilla, and salt in the blender or food processor; blend until smooth.

5. Spoon the filling mixture onto the crust.

6. Cover and freeze for at least 6 hours.

7. Take the cheesecake out of the freezer 1 hour before you'd like to serve it. If you like it softer, continue to let defrost in the refrigerator until the desired consistency is achieved.

STORAGE: Store this pie in an airtight container or wrapped in aluminum foil in the freezer for up to 3 months.

VARIATION TIP: Add ½ cup chopped peanuts or vegan chocolate chips to the pie filling.

Easy Apple Pie

NUT-FREE • SOY-FREE   SERVES: 8

PREP TIME: 20 minutes   REST TIME: 1 hour   COOK TIME: 45 minutes

COOLING TIME: 10 minutes

EQUIPMENT: 9-inch pie pan, large mixing bowl

This simple vegan apple pie will fill your whole house with the aroma of cinnamon. It comes together quickly for a perfect fall dessert.

FOR THE CRUST

1 cup white whole wheat flour, plus more for dusting

½ cup unsweetened applesauce

2 tablespoons coconut sugar

1 teaspoon ground cinnamon

½ teaspoon salt

FOR THE FILLING

3 large apples, cored and thinly sliced (Honeycrisp or Golden Delicious work well)

¼ cup pure maple syrup

2 tablespoons coconut sugar

1 tablespoon ground cinnamon

1. To make the crust: In a large mixing bowl, combine the flour, applesauce, sugar, cinnamon, salt, and 1 tablespoon of water; mix well. Form the dough into a ball, cover, and refrigerate for 1 hour.

2. Preheat the oven to 350°F.

3. In the same large mixing bowl, combine all the filling ingredients and toss until the sliced apples are evenly coated.

4. Dust a sheet of parchment paper with flour. Place the dough ball on the parchment and flatten it into a circle about ⅛ inch thick.

5. Lay the parchment paper with the dough in a 9-inch pie pan.

6. Scoop the apple mixture into the piecrust.

7. Bake for 45 minutes or until the crust is golden brown.

8. Remove the pie from the oven, and let it cool for 10 minutes before slicing and serving.

STORAGE: Store this pie in an airtight container or wrapped in aluminum foil in the refrigerator for up to 5 days.

SERVING TIP: Top your pie slice with a scoop of vegan vanilla ice cream for an extra-delicious treat!

Luscious Pumpkin Pie

SOY-FREE

SERVES: 8

PREP TIME: 20 minutes   COOL TIME: 30 minutes   COOK TIME: 1 hour

COOLING TIME: 15 minutes

EQUIPMENT: 9-inch tart pan, large mixing bowl, blender

I live for pumpkin season, and one reason is this creamy pumpkin pie, one of my favorite pies of all time.

FOR THE CRUST

½ cup quick oats

½ cup whole wheat flour

½ cup coconut sugar

⅓ cup unsweetened applesauce

¼ teaspoon baking soda

¼ teaspoon salt

FOR THE FILLING

1 (15-ounce) can pumpkin purée

½ cup canned chickpeas

½ cup pure maple syrup

½ cup coconut sugar

½ cup raw cashews

1 tablespoon arrowroot starch

2 teaspoons pumpkin pie spice

1 teaspoon pure vanilla extract

1 teaspoon freshly squeezed lemon juice

¼ teaspoon salt

1. Preheat the oven to 375°F. Line a 9-inch tart pan with parchment paper.

2. To make the crust: In a large mixing bowl, combine the oats, flour, sugar, applesauce, baking soda, and salt; mix well.

3. Transfer the crust mixture to the prepared pan and press it evenly into the bottom and sides.

4. Bake for 10 minutes. Set aside to cool for 30 minutes.

5. Reduce the oven heat to 350°F.

6. To make the filling: Combine all the filling ingredients in a blender and blend until smooth.

7. Pour the filling on top of the cooled crust.

8. Bake for 40 to 50 minutes, until the edges of the crust begin to brown.

9. Remove the pie from the oven, and let it cool for 15 minutes before slicing and serving.

STORAGE: Store this pie in an airtight container or wrapped in aluminum foil in the refrigerator for up to 5 days.

SERVING TIP: Top your pie slice with some vegan whipped cream, coconut cream, or a scoop of vegan vanilla ice cream.

Simple Sweet Potato Pie

GLUTEN-FREE • NUT-FREE • SOY-FREE   SERVES: 8

PREP TIME: 15 minutes   FREEZE TIME: 20 minutes   COOK TIME: 45 minutes

COOLING TIME: 15 minutes

EQUIPMENT: 9-inch pie pan, large mixing bowl, high-speed blender or food processor

Though loaded with vitamins, minerals, and fiber, sweet potato pie is, for many people, pumpkin pie's less popular cousin. This easy-to-make recipe might just change its status.

FOR THE CRUST

- 1¼ cups chickpea flour
- 3 tablespoons unsweetened applesauce
- 2 tablespoons pure maple syrup
- 2 tablespoons canned light coconut milk
- 2 tablespoons coconut sugar
- 1 tablespoon ground flaxseed

1. Preheat the oven to 350°F. Line a 9-inch pie pan with parchment paper.

2. To make the crust: In a large mixing bowl, combine the flour, applesauce, maple syrup, coconut milk, sugar, ground flaxseed, and ¼ cup of water; mix well. Cover and freeze for 20 minutes.

3. Meanwhile, combine all the filling ingredients in a high-speed blender or food processor and blend until smooth.

2 cups cooked mashed
cooked sweet potato
(about 1 large
sweet potato)

1 cup canned light
coconut milk

½ cup coconut sugar

¼ cup gluten-free
quick oats

¼ cup unsweetened
applesauce

¼ cup pure maple syrup

1 tablespoon ground
flaxseed

2 teaspoons pure
vanilla extract

1 teaspoon ground
cinnamon

Pinch salt

4. Transfer the chilled crust mixture to the
prepared pan and press it evenly into the
bottom and up the sides.

5. Pour the batter into the crust.

6. Bake for 45 minutes or until the edges of the
crust begin to brown.

7. Remove the pie from the oven, and let it cool
for 15 minutes before slicing and serving.

STORAGE: Store this pie in an airtight container or
wrapped in aluminum foil in the refrigerator for up
to 5 days.

PREP TIP: If you want to bake this crust for another use,
pierce it a few times with a fork. Bake at 350°F for 20 to
25 minutes, until golden brown.

Perfect Pecan Pie

GLUTEN-FREE   SERVES: 8

PREP TIME: 15 minutes   FREEZE TIME: 20 minutes   REFRIGERATION TIME: 20 minutes

COOK TIME: 35 minutes   COOLING TIME: 15 minutes

EQUIPMENT: 9-inch pie pan, two large mixing bowls

Whether you call it "PEE-can" or "pe-KAHN" pie, you'll agree that this pie is perfect.

FOR THE CRUST

1¼ cups chickpea flour

3 tablespoons unsweetened applesauce

2 tablespoons pure maple syrup

2 tablespoons canned light coconut milk

2 tablespoons coconut sugar

1 tablespoon ground flaxseed

FOR THE FILLING

1 cup coconut sugar

2 tablespoons ground flaxseed

½ teaspoon salt

1 cup chopped pecans, plus ½ cup pecan halves for topping

½ cup puréed soft tofu

¼ cup pure maple syrup

1. Preheat the oven to 350°F. Line a 9-inch pie pan with parchment.

2. To make the crust: In a large mixing bowl, combine the flour, applesauce, maple syrup, coconut milk, sugar, ground flaxseed, and ¼ cup of water; mix well. Cover and freeze for 20 minutes.

3. To make the filling: In another large mixing bowl, whisk together the sugar, ground flaxseed, and salt.

4. Add the chopped pecans, tofu, and maple syrup; mix well. Cover and refrigerate for 20 minutes.

5. Transfer the crust to the prepared pie pan and press it evenly into the bottom and sides.

6. Spoon the filling mixture into the piecrust.

7. Top with the pecan halves.

8. Bake for 35 minutes or until the edges of the crust begin to brown.

9. Remove the pie from the oven, and let it cool for 15 minutes before slicing and serving.

STORAGE: Store this pie in an airtight container or wrapped in aluminum foil in the refrigerator for up to 5 days.

SERVING TIP: Top your pie slice with some vegan whipped cream, coconut cream, or a scoop of vegan vanilla ice cream.

Summer Strawberry Tart

GLUTEN-FREE • SOY-FREE • NO-BAKE

SERVES: 8

PREP TIME: 15 minutes

FREEZE TIME: 30 minutes

EQUIPMENT: 9-inch tart pan, high-speed blender or food processor

This beautiful tart screams summer and looks like you've slaved away on it for hours, but it takes only 15 minutes to prepare.

FOR THE CRUST

½ cup raw walnuts

½ cup raw almonds

½ cup unsweetened shredded coconut

¼ cup pure maple syrup

FOR THE FILLING

1 cup raw cashews, soaked in water for 2 hours, then drained

½ cup coconut sugar

½ cup canned chickpeas

¼ cup pure maple syrup

¼ cup canned light coconut milk

2 tablespoons freshly squeezed lemon juice

1 tablespoon pure vanilla extract

1½ cups sliced strawberries

1. Line a 9-inch tart pan with parchment paper.

2. To make the crust: Combine the walnuts, almonds, coconut, and maple syrup in a high-speed blender or food processor; blend until everything is well combined.

3. Transfer the crust mixture to the prepared pan, and use a spatula to press it down evenly into the bottom of the pan.

4. To make the filling: Combine the cashews, sugar, chickpeas, maple syrup, coconut milk, lemon juice, and vanilla in the blender or food processor; blend until smooth.

5. Spoon the filling mixture onto the crust.

6. Place the sliced strawberries on top of the filling, pushing them down so some strawberries are touching the bottom crust.

7. Cover and freeze for at least 30 minutes or refrigerate for at least 2 hours to set.

STORAGE: Store this pie in an airtight container or wrapped in aluminum foil in the refrigerator for up to 5 days or in the freezer for up to 3 months.

VARIATION TIP: Try any fruit you'd like in place of the strawberries—I like to use a combination of blueberries, strawberries, blackberries, and raspberries.

Easy Lemon Tart

GLUTEN-FREE • SOY-FREE • NO-BAKE   SERVES: 8

PREP TIME: 15 minutes   FREEZE TIME: 30 minutes

EQUIPMENT: 7-inch springform pan, high-speed blender or food processor

This tangy vegan tart is sure to be loved by all. Take it to the pool or beach and dive in!

FOR THE CRUST

½ cup raw walnuts

½ cup raw almonds

½ cup unsweetened shredded coconut

¼ cup pure maple syrup

FOR THE FILLING

1 cup raw cashews, soaked in water for 2 hours, then drained

½ cup coconut sugar

½ cup canned chickpeas

Grated zest of 1 lemon

½ cup freshly squeezed lemon juice

¼ cup pure maple syrup

1 tablespoon pure vanilla extract

1. Line a 7-inch springform pan with parchment paper.

2. To make the crust: Combine the walnuts, almonds, coconut, and maple syrup in a high-speed blender or food processor; blend until everything is well combined.

3. Transfer the crust mixture to the prepared pan, and use a spatula to press it down evenly into the bottom of the pan.

4. Combine all the filling ingredients in the blender or food processor and blend until smooth.

5. Spoon the filling mixture onto the crust.

6. Cover and freeze for at least 30 minutes or refrigerate for at least 2 hours to set.

STORAGE: Store this pie in an airtight container or wrapped in aluminum foil in the refrigerator for up to 5 days or in the freezer for up to 3 months.

VARIATION TIP: Make this a tropical tart by adding some diced pineapple before freezing. Make sure to press the pineapple down into the filling.

The Dirty Dozen™ and the Clean Fifteen™

A nonprofit environmental watchdog organization called Environmental Working Group (EWG) looks at data supplied by the US Department of Agriculture (USDA) and the Food and Drug Administration (FDA) about pesticide residues. Each year it compiles a list of the best and worst pesticide loads found in commercial crops. You can use these lists to decide which fruits and vegetables to buy organic to minimize your exposure to pesticides and which produce is considered safe enough to buy conventionally. This does not mean they are pesticide-free, though, so wash these fruits and vegetables thoroughly. The list is updated annually, and you can find it online at EWG.org/FoodNews.

DIRTY DOZEN™

1. strawberries
2. spinach
3. kale
4. nectarines
5. apples
6. grapes
7. peaches
8. cherries
9. pears
10. tomatoes
11. celery
12. potatoes

CLEAN FIFTEEN™

1. avocados
2. sweet corn*
3. pineapples
4. sweet peas (frozen)
5. onions
6. papayas*
7. eggplants
8. asparagus
9. kiwis
10. cabbages
11. cauliflower
12. cantaloupes
13. broccoli
14. mushrooms
15. honeydew melons

* A small amount of sweet corn and papaya sold in the United States is produced from genetically modified seeds. Buy organic varieties of these crops if you want to avoid genetically modified produce.

Measurement Conversions

	US STANDARD	US STANDARD (OUNCES)	METRIC (APPROXIMATE)
VOLUME EQUIVALENTS (LIQUID)	2 tablespoons	1 fl. oz.	30 mL
	¼ cup	2 fl. oz.	60 mL
	½ cup	4 fl. oz.	120 mL
	1 cup	8 fl. oz.	240 mL
	1½ cups	12 fl. oz.	355 mL
	2 cups or 1 pint	16 fl. oz.	475 mL
	4 cups or 1 quart	32 fl. oz.	1 L
	1 gallon	128 fl. oz.	4 L
VOLUME EQUIVALENTS (DRY)	⅛ teaspoon		0.5 mL
	¼ teaspoon		1 mL
	½ teaspoon		2 mL
	¾ teaspoon		4 mL
	1 teaspoon		5 mL
	1 tablespoon		15 mL
	¼ cup		59 mL
	⅓ cup		79 mL
	½ cup		118 mL
	⅔ cup		156 mL
	¾ cup		177 mL
	1 cup		235 mL
	2 cups or 1 pint		475 mL
	3 cups		700 mL
	4 cups or 1 quart		1 L
	½ gallon		2 L
	1 gallon		4 L
WEIGHT EQUIVALENTS	½ ounce		15 g
	1 ounce		30 g
	2 ounces		60 g
	4 ounces		115 g
	8 ounces		225 g
	12 ounces		340 g
	16 ounces or 1 pound		455 g

	FAHRENHEIT (F)	CELSIUS (C) (APPROXIMATE)
OVEN TEMPERATURES	250°F	120°F
	300°F	150°C
	325°F	180°C
	375°F	190°C
	400°F	200°C
	425°F	220°C
	450°F	230°C

Weights of Common Whole Food Baking Ingredients

INGREDIENT	VOLUME	WEIGHT
Cocoa powder (unsweetened)	1 tablespoon	5 grams
Almond flour	¼ cup	28 grams
Chickpea flour	¼ cup	30 grams
Coconut flour	¼ cup	30 grams
Oat flour	⅓ cup	30 grams
Spelt flour	¼ cup	30 grams
White whole wheat flour	¼ cup	30 grams
Whole wheat flour	¼ cup	30 grams
Quick oats	½ cup	40 grams
Peanut butter	2 tablespoons	32 grams
Ground chia seeds	1 tablespoon	12 grams
Ground flaxseed	1 tablespoon	6.5 grams
Coconut sugar	1 tablespoon	12 grams
Maple syrup	¼ cup	340 grams

Ingredient Substitutions

CONVENTIONAL BAKING INGREDIENT	WHOLE FOOD SUBSTITUTION
1 stick butter	½ cup unsweetened applesauce
	½ cup pumpkin purée
	½ cup mashed avocado
	½ cup mashed canned chickpeas
	½ cup puréed soft tofu
	½ cup nut butter
	1 tablespoon ground flaxseed + 3 tablespoons water
1 large egg	1 tablespoon ground flaxseed + 3 tablespoons water
	¼ cup unsweetened applesauce
	¼ cup mashed banana
	¼ cup pumpkin purée
	¼ cup mashed avocado
	¼ cup puréed soft tofu
	3 tablespoons nut or seed butter
1 large egg white	3 tablespoons aquafaba (liquid from a can of chickpeas)
1 cup oil	1 cup unsweetened applesauce
	1 cup pumpkin purée
	1 cup mashed avocado
	1 cup mashed canned chickpeas
	1 cup puréed soft tofu
	1 cup nut butter

CONVENTIONAL BAKING INGREDIENT	WHOLE FOOD SUBSTITUTION
1 cup cow's milk	1 cup unsweetened almond milk
	1 cup unsweetened rice milk
	1 cup unsweetened soy milk
	1 cup unsweetened cashew milk
1 cup buttermilk	1 cup unsweetened soy milk + 1 teaspoon freshly squeezed lemon juice
1 cup condensed milk	1 cup canned full-fat coconut milk
1 cup honey	1 cup maple syrup
	1 cup agave
1 cup yogurt	1 cup vegan yogurt
1 cup sugar	1 cup coconut sugar

INGREDIENT SUBSTITUTIONS FOR RECIPES USED IN THIS BOOK

INGREDIENT	SUBSTITUTION
1 tablespoon ground flaxseed	1 tablespoon ground chia seeds
1 cup whole wheat flour	1 cup white whole wheat flour
	1 cup spelt flour
	⅞ cup (14 tablespoons) chickpea flour
1 cup oat flour	1½ cups quick or rolled oats ground into flour
½ cup unsweetened applesauce	½ cup pumpkin purée
	½ cup mashed banana
½ cup puréed soft tofu	½ cup mashed canned chickpeas
½ cup maple syrup	½ cup agave
½ cup peanut butter	½ cup almond butter
	½ cup sunflower seed butter
½ cup vegan chocolate chips	½ cup raisins
	½ cup chopped nuts

Index

Acknowledgments

First and foremost, I'd like to thank Callisto Media for making the publication of this cookbook possible, and for giving me the incredible opportunity to share my love of whole food, plant-based baking with the world.

I'd also like to thank my parents, Susan and Michael Markowitz, who are my number one supporters and biggest fans. They have been with me every step of the way, cheering me on and guiding me, not only through this book writing process, but through my entire life. They are the most incredible role models of unconditional love, perseverance, and compassion. I love you so much, Mom and Dad!

About the Author

Dr. Annie Markowitz is a weight loss expert, wellness coach, and founder of the popular recipe website, VegAnnie.com. Her love for health and wellness began when she discovered the plant-based lifestyle in college, which helped her lose over 75 pounds and led her to pursuing and obtaining her PhD in nutrition from the University of Texas at Austin. She is passionate about helping others achieve a healthy, sustainable lifestyle that will lead to a long, happy life!

CPSIA information can be obtained
at www.ICGtesting.com
Printed in the USA
LVHW011810221020
669407LV00004B/8